Secrets of Selling
to
Retailers and Wholesalers

Peter Kemp

For James and Nathaniel.
May they successfully sell themselves in life.

Published by RTC Books
Index House, Ascot SL5 5ET UK

ISBN-13: 978-1479113095
ISBN-10: 1479113093

Index House, Ascot SL5 7ET UK

ABOUT THIS BOOK

This is a complete guide to selling consumer products to the retail and wholesale trades. In particular it is designed for those who have never had the advantage of a training course in salesmanship.

This manual will also inspire self-employed sales people who require some extra advice and expertise to sell their product or service more effectively.

You may be attracted to the idea of selling as a potential career. Here you will learn everything you need to know about the art of salesmanship.

In particular, we will improve the skills of all those involved with the marketing and selling of fast moving consumer goods (FMCG).

This is, also a sales training course for anyone working for a small or medium sized company that may not have sufficient resources to operate a meaningful on-going sales training programme.

This course will help you develop more profitable selling techniques; you will learn how to get bigger and better orders, and, how to earn bigger commission cheques,

We will be covering all the secrets of selling consumer goods to the retail trade and you will learn

- How to be a better salesman,
- How to manage your territory
- How to overcome objections,
- How to close that sale,
- How to go prospecting,
- How to handle complaints,

You will discover a host of tips and techniques that allow you to turn in a consistently better sales performance.

In short this study course is guaranteed to help you develop the skills required in your chosen sales career, and to become a better salesperson.

CONTENTS

Preface	Introducing the Sales Person	5
Chapter 1	Managing your territory	12
Chapter 2	Maintaining Sales Records	19
Chapter 3	Secrets of Basic Salesmanship	24
Chapter 4	Building your Sales presentation	34
Chapter 5	The Pre-Presentation Check-List	41
Chapter 6	Buying Motives	43
Chapter 7	Polishing your Performance	47
Chapter 8	Objections and How to Overcome Them	50
Chapter 9	Closing the Sale	65
Chapter 10	Analyse that Presentation	74
Chapter11	Prospecting	77
Chapter12	Opening a New Account	84
Chapter13	Opening and Closing a Credit Account	86
Chapter14	Credit Control and Cash Collections	88
Chapter15	How to Handle Complaints	90
Chapter16	The Wholesaler & Retailer Relationship	92
Chapter17	Merchandising your products	94
Chapter 18	Finally	100

PREFACE

INTRODUCING THE SALES PERSON

Let us start by examining the world of the Sales Person.

There was a time when this very thought would conjure up an image of a fast talking, foot in the door, confidence trickster, whose main aim in life was to entice you to part with your hard earned cash, and give you little, if nothing, in return.

Those days are now history. Indeed, that totally inaccurate perception of the sales person has, thankfully, gone forever. Today's sales people are totally dedicated professionals that provide a vital link in the overall chain of supply; and are an indispensable contact between the producer of goods or services, through the distribution chain, and on to the ultimate customer.

But, imagine, if you will, living in a world where there are no sales people. Just what sort of place would that be? If you give it some thought then the obvious conclusion is that without sales people we would find ourselves living a very primitive existence. And a pretty dull one at that.

Just consider this. If the economic system that we enjoy today is to survive then we will always need sales people to keep the wheels of commerce and industry turning.

But more than simply requiring a large number of sales people, what our commercial world really needs is an abundance of 'Salesmanship. And professional selling in all its many various guises.

Just look around you. The chances are that everything you can see has, somewhere along the line, been sold by one person to another on at least one occasion. And, hopefully, for a profit.

Every product that was ever manufactured and the many thousands of inventions and innovations that today form an integral part of our daily life and its environment. All those countless objects, possessions and services around our home and work-place that we now take totally for granted. They all had to be sold before they could ever be used or enjoyed by us.

We must also accept that selling, and the art of salesmanship has to exist at many different levels and it touches both our personal and our business lives. And whether we realise it or not we are all, in effect, salesmen. And each of us will, in one form or another, experience some aspect of salesmanship during every waking day.

Let us now discuss just a few examples of salesmanship in action. Whenever we make a purchase, whether it is a product or a service, we have either directly or indirectly, been sold to. In turn we will need to use salesmanship whenever we wish to influence another person to our way of thinking. We will experience salesmanship whenever someone succeeds in influencing us. Advertising is selling. Politics is all about the selling of thoughts, ideas, and policies. Indeed, we all have to sell ourselves whenever we feel the need to create the right impression, or to advance a cause or idea.

The simple and basic truth is that we cannot escape from selling, from salesmanship or, for that matter, from sales people.

I believe that this clearly demonstrates that selling is a totally necessary component, not only of trade and industry, but to our basic and normal way of life.

Above all, selling is a career that is followed by millions of men and women and as such is one of the most exciting and rewarding professions that could possibly be pursued.

Selling has just about everything to offer the ambitious. It's all there for the asking - the thrill of the chase, and a genuine satisfaction of achievement.

In short - personal success.

Selling is a life full of excitement. Every day will bring a fresh challenge; a new experience and another business opportunity to be exploited. And, at the same time, a career in sales can offer really tremendous financial rewards. To the right person. And by that I mean to the person that has been well trained, and is constantly concerned about developing and sharpening up their own basic selling skills.

At this point there is something that I want to make absolutely clear. And it is this. Any discussion on the role of the salesman will beg the age old question: Is a Salesman born or made?

Sure, there are those that appear to have what is often scornfully called "the gift of the gab." You will meet plenty of these in the selling profession, but I firmly believe that the answer to this question is that the most successful Salespeople are those that have been *trained* to sell.

Those very large companies that operate in the field of consumer goods, companies that are the size of say, Proctor & Gamble, The Mars Company or Cadbury/Schweppes, operate very sophisticated sales training programmes. They prefer to mould raw recruits into their own tried and trusted methods of selling.

This 'in-house' training is very sophisticated, and a very high percentage of the top Salesmen around today have broken into sales this way. Also it is mainly the larger companies that have the resources to send their employees on the many hundreds of sales training courses that are held annually all over the country.

These major corporations can provide a modern sales training programme that is comprehensive, and they have a sales force that is kept up to date with the latest thinking and expertise.

Any prospective consumer goods salesman would really be well advised to consider the benefits of beginning his selling career with such a large, national or international organisation.

But, obviously and realistically, such start to a sales career cannot be possible or even feasible for the vast majority of Salesmen, many of whom will have to learn the craft the hard was – on the job.

However it is not just the professional salesperson that needs to continually update and improve his techniques.

I believe that everyone involved in business, in any capacity whatsoever, will need to acquire some basic degree of skill in selling and salesmanship to be totally successful.

Whether one is primarily concerned with administration, credit control or production there is a huge advantage to be gained, both by you, and your employers, in being sales orientated. A sales orientated employee knows that in business the customer is KING and that his ability to improve on the Company's relationship with its customers will increase, not only his employer's overall profitability, but will also have the positive effect of dramatically enhancing his own chances of future promotion and career advancement.

Consequently this course will also help anyone employed in a non-selling career who believes that they will have a distinct advantage in becoming more sales orientated and having a greater awareness of salesmanship. If this is you, then this manual will definitely bring real benefits to you.

So, if you do fall into any of these categories, or indeed, if you are currently considering the prospect of a career in sales, then this course is also for you.

Now read on and together we will develop and widen your basic, albeit latent, selling skills. Then, if you can put what you learn into practice, you will become a really true professional. The sky could be your limit. Your sales ability could well take you around the world, and all the way to the top job in the boardroom. That's what selling has done for me, and it's exactly what selling can do for you. It's all there for the asking.

This course will now start right at the bottom-most rung of the sales ladder. So let's get back to basics.

Remember, it is from this very first moment that you will have to adopt those skills and habits that, once learned, will soon become second nature to you. And these skills will then last you the whole of your lifetime.

And even if you have been 'on the road' for some considerable time and have acquired this book out of curiosity, why not join me on this exciting journey. Yes, it will take you back to the fundamental basics, but now this could well be the best time for you to re-learn everything again right from scratch. And who knows, in doing so you might just discover something that is novel or new to you.

You may even find something that will work effectively for you.

Library shelves are full of books on salesmanship. Most are first rate, but they all have one basic fault. It seems to me that they have all been written with the industrial or speciality salesman in mind.

Much of what has been written for industrial sales people is irrelevant to the job that you will have to do. At best you may well learn something new, but it is unlikely that these publications will teach you how to successfully cope with many of those particular problems and quirks that are unique to the retail trade.

Learning how to negotiate a million pound contract is one thing. The selling of industrial and speciality products and services really does require very special knowledge and skill.

But such expertise does not necessarily enable you to successfully cope with a 9.00 am appointment at a local newsagent's shop.

So, first of all let us take just a short look at the real world of the FMCG salesperson.

Image this scene.

You are fresh; it is your very first call of the day. You are raring to go and you are full of enthusiasm.

Your customer, on the other hand, has been up since 4 o'clock. Two of his paper boys have failed to turn up for work; since 7 am he had had a procession of customers moaning about the weather, the price of cigarettes, and complaining that they received the wrong newspaper.

By 9 o'clock your buyer has yet to find the time to shave, to grab a cup of coffee, or even to have a decent breakfast.

Then, in walks some 'smart Alec' salesperson trying to sell him some special Christmas line: and here we are in the middle of May.

Do you get the picture?

The points that we shall discuss during this course will equip you with the ability to meet this type of situation with tact, with understanding, and with a firm determination to win that order.

This programme will provide you with many of those tricks of the trade that will turn a mere order taker into a top flight consumer goods salesman.

I would now like to invite you to enjoy the world of the consumer products Salesman. My hope is that this course will make a major contribution to your future success.

I know that you can do it. In fact, we can do it – together.

Let us now start on your very own special programme for self advancement and self improvement through salesmanship.

You may well find that your chosen career becomes a success beyond your wildest dreams.

You are definitely destined to become a better sales person, so let us get straight down to business.

CHAPTER 1

MANAGING YOUR TERRITORY

This could be the biggest day in your life. You have your very own sales area or territory and everything about it is new and strange. The first thing you will discover is that this new territory is either one of the Company's better areas in terms of sales volume, or one of the worst. *Either way you are going to win.*

In taking over a profitable, well managed territory you will undoubtedly be able to bring a fresh approach and outlook to that area, and very soon you will be able to exploit all those new selling situations and opportunities that actually were there all along, but were missed by your predecessor. If, however you have a virgin, or even worse, a run down territory, then the only way you can possible go is UP. The opportunities that exist for you are truly enormous. **You have just got to believe.**

The expert salesman just cannot lose. And this is especially true when you know where to look. And YOU soon will.

But, before we can get down to discuss those profitable selling techniques in any great detail we must, first take a good look at the essential planning and preparation that has to be done before you can make any really productive sales call.

And the first lesson that you will need to learn is this.

Every sales person is, if he is anything, a Territory Manager.

And I want you to make no mistake about this. The ultimate success of every sales territory will depend not only on the actual sales made, but on just how well the area is managed. In fact, I believe that the major difference between an average, middle of the road salesman, and the high-flying star that really does a fantastic selling job, is not his overall sales ability and experience. It's often not even his call rate or his sparkling personality.

Overall success largely depends on your ability to be a good territory manager.

A manager that will take full responsibility for managing his time, managing his appointments, as well as managing the overall sales growth of his territory.

There are two important points to highlight here.

- *Remember that every business aspect of the territory has to be covered,*
- *and every call you make must be planned in detail.*

GET TO KNOW YOUR TERRITORY

I have always believed that the one absolutely fundamental aspect of good territory management is a thorough and intimate knowledge of your sales area. And I would include knowing exactly those parts of the area that will need your extra special attention. By the way, there is no rule that says you have to cover the whole of your territory and every single possible outlet. *But you must work on developing those vital parts and those customers that can really justify your valuable time. And, indeed, those customers or prospects that really have a meaningful potential for future sales growth.*

But, if we are going to start at the beginning we must first learn some local geography. And the best way to learn the geography of your area is to invest in a good, large scale, up-to-date map. The best map is the kind that opens up flat so that it can easily be covered with clear plastic film or sheeting. The map could be mounted onto a board or wooden base for greater efficiency. Now you are ready for action.

Take a felt-tip or marker pen and clearly outline the area's boundaries. Now add some of the more important landmarks, not forgetting to include such features as major new shopping developments, as well as, what might be a life-saving tip - public conveniences.

Now mark out all your business calls. I prefer to stick different coloured pins into the map that highlight

- All the current live accounts
- Potentially good prospect calls
- All major competitor's accounts

All your current account customers should be categorised by their full sales potential, and also by the number of calls you will need to make if you are to achieve your set sales objectives.

This map should also show the market coverage that you currently enjoy, and all the other possible opportunities for future development.

You should be able to see at a glance those weaker areas that would obviously benefit from extra effort when you are prospecting for new business. As you record more and more information on the map you will start to see how well your sales penetration of the area is developing.

PLAN YOUR TERRITORY

All your regular and your prospect calls should now pinned out on your territory map. Each day's journey plan can now be properly organized. One simple, but useful method of journey planning is to take a piece of string and draw loops around each of the calls that you wish to make that day. Bearing in mind that you are unlikely to get it right first time, or even every time, perhaps it might be smart to use a marker pen to make out a rough route, and then you can easily make changes as you continue to develop your journey plan.

Your final objective however is to find the shortest journey that will allow you to take in all your calls while allowing you extra time on route for those all important prospect calls.

To sum up, you need a map mounted with clear plastic upon which

- *You can pin or mark all your calls.*

- *You can categorise your customers by the number of calls in each journey cycle.*

There you have it. A basis for planning your work.

Your maxim should now be.

PLAN YOUR WORK AND WORK YOUR PLAN

PLAN YOUR CALLS

There really is only one simple reason for basic route planning, and it is this. Route planning will enable you to achieve the highest number of orders set against the lowest amount of time and expense. That's not only sound economics but good business practice.

The frequency of every call must also be a vital factor in your journey plan. You should be deciding on just how often during every journey cycle each of your customers or prospects will need to be visited.

Your most frequent calls should be made on:-

- *Those larger customers that are already giving you substantial orders and which project a sustained future growth pattern.*
- *Major customers that are currently placing smaller orders but have the potential for expanding the business that they actually do with you and your Company.*
- *All other customers or prospective customers that appear to have real potential. This category must certainly include those buyers who are currently major accounts for the competition, and this is especially important for those businesses that are progressive and have strong management teams.*

You can make less frequent calls, or better still, cut out altogether, accounts that:-

- *Order small unprofitable amounts, and have no real scope or inclination to increase the business that they could do with you.*
- *Are poor credit risks, or give you the impression that they are poor housekeepers.*
- *Do not properly merchandise, display, or handle your products, and give the impression of having very little motivation to do so.*

Only by highlighting all those obviously unprofitable calls and ruthlessly weeding them out will you ever be able to devote sufficient time to your major customers and still have time left over for prospecting new business.

Now that all your calls and prospect calls are included on your territory map, you can now plan your call routes in the most efficient manner.

However, managing your territory and your sales calls is only part of the job.

You now have to learn to
- *Manage your time*
- *Manage your appointments*
- *Manage your Sales Growth*

MANAGE YOUR TIME

I have already said successful territory management will, to a large extent, depend on how good you are at managing your time. Time is the enemy of us all and this is especially true of everyone in sales. But once you have discovered how best to manage your own time you will be well on your way. Indeed you would then have solved one of the biggest problems that you are ever likely to have.

Remember – time is not only a most costly commodity, but its misuse is certainly one of the world's most expensive luxuries.

Of course, these statements equally apply to many other aspects of your life, but I must stress this point for one simple reason. *In our profession a sale can be won or lost in the short time that it takes to blink an eye.* And there's more. Time saved can mean an extra call or even an extra order. That, in itself, justifies making every effort to minimise, and eliminate, any obvious time wasting.

So, whenever you think that you have insufficient time just ask yourself a number of probing and pertinent questions. Answer honestly and you will soon find that you can quickly improve the level of your own working efficiency. The replies that you give to some basic questions will enable you to work on the more productive aspects of the job that will, in turn, encourage you to cut out most of those activities that are essentially a serious waste of your valuable time.

It sounds trite I know, but I make no apology for making the following obvious statement.

It is always going to be a lot easier to save a few minutes here, and an extra few minutes there than it will ever be to find a vital couple of extra hours in a day.

Sounds obvious? Yes, but I guarantee that a number of your competitors will be falling into this time wasting trap, and this is not a mistake that you are going to make. Is it?

Let us now try to see where you can actually save some of that wasted or lost time and dramatically improve your work rate.

First of all check that you are using all that time spent behind the wheel of your car in an efficient and profitable manner. Are you just meandering along while enjoying the view, or are you using your driving time to mentally prepare yourself for the next call, while keeping a sharp lookout for any new business opportunities that could come your way?

Next; give serious consideration to what should be done about those customers that actually allow you to waste your time.

In other words, you need to work on reducing the time you spend with any contact that, in the final analysis, is really unable to influence the final buying situation?

As we discussed earlier you must reduce, or cut out altogether any calls that can only ever order small, unprofitable amounts; do not properly represent your line; or are poor credit risks.

And also ask yourself this - are you working on avoiding some or all of that unproductive chit-chat which you so frequently find yourself engaged in?

Finally, remember this:-
Time can only be used once, and has to be used the very first moment that it comes into your possession.

MAKING AND MANAGING APPOINTMENTS

A regular appointment system is a must for every professional; it is therefore a must for you (the note introducing the next chapter is relevant here).

And, if you already have your own appointment system, it is really important that you give serious thought as to what steps can be taken to improve it?

Operating a good appointment system means that you will always know where you are going and where you are due next. And this is even more important; *a firm appointment means that your buyer will be anticipating your call,* and if he knows when to expect you, he may well have his regular repeat order ready and waiting, thus saving you even more time.

By the way, if you are ever worried about making appointments, don't be.   A simple and easy method is to get your buyer to agree on a time for your next call *– before you leave your present one.*   Another method is to telephone your customer beforehand – and just ask for an appointment.

It seems that actually asking for an appointment does worry some people.   But it shouldn't. You already know the date when you are next due to visit the area, so check out what times are convenient to you. Then suggest a time and date that suits you, and rather than risking him choosing a difficult time for you, give him the choice between two alternatives – with a positive answer suiting you both equally.

Never ask "What day would suit you, Mr. Buyer?" Rather suggest alternatives that would suit you. Ask *"Would you prefer Tuesday or Wednesday?"*

Also never ask "What time?" Instead suggest, *"Morning or afternoon?",* and then perhaps ask *"3 o'clock or 4 o'clock?"*

In other words, you always make it easy for the buyer to decide on what actually suits you best. That is the easiest way to get an appointment.

But now that you do have an appointment you must now make sure that you honour it to the minute.

MANAGING YOUR SALES GROWTH

To properly manage the area's sales growth means that you will be systematically analysing all the available and current sales data that can be gleaned from your sales area or territory, and you will readily see what has already been achieved on the area. You are now in a strong position to see exactly what needs to be done to increase sales even further.

The next step is to find a method of maintaining the territory's current sales volume, as well as planning for real and sustained future sales growth.

You will soon come to realise that there are basically only two ways in which you can increase the sales volume from your area.
- **You can increase sales from your existing customer accounts.**
- **You can find new customers.**

Increase Sales from Current Customers

You will do this by constantly introducing new lines and by gradually improving the overall sales from each and every one of your customers. It is important to the overall success of your area that you constantly ask yourself this question. *"Am I getting as much business as possible from this customer, or is he going elsewhere for products that he could just as easily obtain from me?"*

Clearly you will need to make sure that all your existing customers are squeezed for every drop of business going. But here is a warning. Never forget that it is all too easy, especially when you have just taken an order for repeat sales, that, having reached your Company's minimum order level, you breathe a sigh of relief, and then beat a hasty retreat out of the store before the buyer changes his mind. It's an easy and understandable attitude to take.   After all, you did get the order. But this is the reaction of the order taker. To improve the sales from all your existing customers.

You can offer customers those established and well proven products that they are not currently stocking, and you can help them to increase sales through improved merchandising.

Find new customers
Although it is absolutely vital to increase sales from your current customer base, make no mistake about this.

You may well find it time consuming, but **the most important and profitable source of any real sales growth on your area will most likely come from NEW business.**

Once you understand this, you will also understand the tremendous importance of devoting a sizeable and realistic amount of your time to prospecting for new business. Later you will find a whole Chapter devoted to the art of prospecting, where we will discuss this very important subject in greater depth.

Remember
I want you to become as familiar with your territory as you are with your own back garden and then this thorough and intimate knowledge of your sales area and its geography will ensure that no new sales opportunities are missed.

So there you have it. And to sum up all we have covered in this Chapter, I will repeat that to be a true professional at managing your territory you must
- *Get to know your territory*
- *Plan your territory*
- *Plan calls*
- *Manage your time*
- *Make appointments*
- *Manage sales growth*

And finally remember that plans mean nothing until they are enacted.

PLAN YOUR WORK AND WORK YOUR PLAN

CHAPTER 2

RECORDS

An introductory note

It is essential that you keep accurate records, and computers are there to help you.

That is what computers do. Some people have photographic memories but most of us have to write things down if we are not to forget important orders, times, dates and details. Computers are helpful and many companies will require that their sales people use a device to keep their records in a file which can be easily accessed by both you and your back office. This is sensible because the data that is collected can be useful in many ways both for the sales person and for the company.

However, if this were a book about writing a novel it would not include a great deal about the word processing facilities of a computer. Consequently I will not go into computer data in depth.

The computer has now been integrated into our lives but it is only a means to an end: the principles of selling are not affected by the way in which records are kept. This book emphasises the importance of records and they are vital *but the format is irrelevant* so the advice given here is not interrupted and complicated by a detailed analysis of the technology that is required of many salesman on the road today

If the company for which you work does not provide this technological backup or you are a self-employed representative, the methods described are perfectly adequate using pen, paper and notebooks but there are tremendous advantages in using a computer programme. This does not have to be expensive and in fact if you log onto:

http://www.reallysimplesystems.com

You can sign up to an excellent (and free) Customer Relationship Management (CRM) system which is likely to fulfil all your needs. There is an excellent training video and good programme support on their web site.

Even if you are not particularly computer literate and though it might look a complicated to start with, if you give it a little time the process and principles quickly become clear. The programme has the advantage of doing your analysis for you and will notify you of any calls or deadlines which are important.

Putting in the initial information takes a more time than writing it down but you only ever have to do it once and the program will not only keep all your prospects in order and up-to-date but create 'to-do lists' and reminders so you are prompted by the system so clients are contacted when they expect you to do so.

This is not to say that a simple written record system does not work perfectly well but technology ensures that all your notes are complete and *legible*!

However you keep records the principles of selling product to retailers does not change and that is the process on which this book focuses.

MAINTAINING YOUR RECORDS

I have said it before, but I still think it is well worth repeating.

Often the major difference between someone who will merely do an average job, and a salesman that is a top performer, is primarily the ability to organise his work.

And, in my view, the maintenance of a complete set of sales records is a fundamental adjunct to professional salesmanship.

Sales records are not just an invaluable aid but, when used intelligently, will provide you and your company with a wealth of vital data.

And we include information such as customer profiles: an analysis of past sales results: current and future trends: and much more.

Your records should be able to tell you everything that you need to know to enable you to produce that all important slice of sales volume.

If you are currently working for a well organised company, you may have already been issued with a complete set of sales records. Use them and keep them up to date.

If such records are not already supplied, you will be well advised to develop a set of your own.

You must never look at record keeping as unproductive or company red tape or even as a chore, but rather as a necessary tool that will assist you in working towards a more positive and constructive selling job.

Certainly all this is extra work, but without question, it is worth every bit of the extra effort.

A full set of records will reward you more than ten times over, and like me, you will soon be wondering just how any salesman could survive without them.

The basic records that you need to keep are quite simple. In addition to your territory map, you should provide yourself with the following:

1) A set of Customer Account Cards

A customer account card, which may be on your laptop or handheld computer of course but we will stack to the principles here and use paper to demonstrate them sp the account card need only be a plain piece of white or manila card and should be designed so that it can show a complete pen-picture of your customer and his buying habits. All the information that you would ever need to know about the customer must be recorded and then continually kept up to date.
Such information should include

- *The customer's name, address, telephone number etc.*
- *The delivery address*
- *The account number*
- *The type of outlet (wholesaler/retailer)*
- *The best time to see and normal opening hours.*
- *The type of merchandise stocked (are any competitive lines stocked?)*
- *Customer's history (date account opened, etc.)*
- *Personal matters (items that indicate to the buyer that you are interested in him personally as well as being a business contact.*

Your records should then be filed in journey order. These account cards will serve as an invaluable means of remembering all those important details about your customer. And there is a bonus. - kept up to date, a good set of account cards will make it so much easier to organise our journey plan.

2) Customer Coverage Charts

Another useful tool that you should never be without is what I would call a "Coverage Chart". This should be designed so that you can record, in product order, full details of all the past business that has been received from the customer. In other words the Coverage Chart should list all those products that are currently being stocked by this account, with details of the overall sales volume. You can then use this information to help you to sell on every single call.
In short, a good coverage chart will provide you with all the facts that you will need if you are to sell all the products in the range, and it should also provide you with the information that will allow you to increase each order over the previous one.

3) Customer Call Reports

Whether you have to complete it daily, weekly or monthly, your Customer Call

Report is another vital aid that will improve your ability to sell more. However, I know that some sales people will simply look upon Call Reports as a method that Sales Managers have of checking up on them. You will not make this mistake.

If you report to a Sales Manager you will know that every Sales Manager will need certain information that can only be supplied by you. This information will provide him and the Company with an overall picture of all the sales areas under his control.

Even if you are self-employed you will realise that, in addition, call reports will be of enormous help. They will tell you the number of calls made on each journey; the effectiveness of those calls; and the products that were sold.

Further, a call report will highlight your strengths and weaknesses; and will give you some indication as to your current position with regard to your set sales target.

4) Order Forms

No discussion on sales reports and administration would be complete without some mention of the most important form of all. **The Order Form.** In many organisations a duplicate copy of the order form is used by the packing department and another copy by the accounts department for the raising of invoices.

Be careless when completing an order form and you've got problems. The customer may get the wrong order, or even an incorrect invoice. What you will get is the blame.

Take care to fill in your Order Form legibly, clearly and correctly.

IN SUMMARY

I have heard some so-called salesmen say that if they did not have to spend so much time on paperwork, they would have the time to be able to make more calls. So they might, but there is no way in which these calls can be as well prepared, as effective or as profitable as those calls made by a true professional who has done his homework. And a true professional is what you are. Without doubt, good administration is part and parcel of being a professional salesman.

The more information that you have at your fingertips, then more effective will be your selling ability. Research has shown that continuous up-to-date information increases a salesman's output. Every time.

You now understand that all sales records must be carefully and actuarially kept and they must at least include:-

- *A complete set of customer account files*

- *A set of coverage charts.*
- *Daily, weekly or monthly call reports.*
- *Adequate Supplies of Order forms*

You now have the basis of a good foundation course for the real professional. Good territory knowledge, practical route planning, and the maintenance of a full set of informative sales records. In short firstly you must become a good all-round administrator. Then, and only then, can you possibly begin to develop your skills in the art of selling.

CHAPTER 3

BASIC SALESMANSHIP

You now have an appreciation of the importance of total territory knowledge, work planning and good basic administration. Your next step is to develop the techniques that you will require to 'sell yourself'. At least 'selling yourself' is how the unenlightened man in the street might well describe salesmanship. But it's not as simple as that.

It is my firm belief that long before you can sell yourself, as well as your Company and its products, you must first create the right selling atmosphere. In other words, the correct business relationship must exist between yourself and the buyer. Indeed, a friendly and positive selling environment must always be present. This is the only way I know of "selling yourself". It's the overall selling environment that you create that is important, not your irresistible personality and charm.

THE SELLING ENVIRONMENT

To create an 'ideal selling environment' is not the easiest thing in the world. But it's not too difficult either.

There are basically just four simple ingredients that go towards creating this ideal selling situation, so you should be able to quickly grasp the basic ground rules, and then learn to follow them instinctively.

To create the ideal selling environment you must:-

- *Cultivate a friendly relationship between yourself and the buyer.*
- *Use your ability to increase the buyer's self esteem.*
- *Use your ability to gain the buyer's confidence.*
- *Use your talent for showing sincere enthusiasm.*

Let us now look at each one of these ingredients a little more closely.

1) Cultivate a friendly relationship

Until you are able to cultivate a sincere, friendly, and genuine relationship between yourself and the buyer you will clearly experience a number of problems. Indeed, you may not even get off the starting grid. Although nobody is really happy about doing business with someone they dislike, let me say at the outset that the salesperson that is popular with every one of his customers is yet to be born. From time to time, and by the very nature of things, we will all rub someone up the wrong way. So let's be sensible and realistic. This is not such a major problem for the industrial or speciality salesman. He has to create a good first impression that's true, and he has to sure that his personality does not interfere or conflict with his sales presentation. In doing his job professionally he will ensure that his product, as well as the product's features and unique selling points are highlighted and projected into the buyer's mind. In the world of industrial or speciality selling it is important that only a totally business like relationship exists between the seller and the buyer.

On the other hand you are selling consumer goods to the wholesaler and to the retailer. Yours is a world where the "one-off" sale does not exist. Having sold him once, you will have to have to return to this same customer time and time again to obtain those profitable repeat sales and to introduce further new lines. You might have to return every week, every month or every quarter depending on the level of business generated. But return you must. And therefore in your situation it is simply not enough to create a good first impression. All your efforts must be directed towards creating a totally on-going friendly atmosphere. A business-like relationship certainly, but in addition a special type of friendship, a positive empathy even, has to exist between you and your customer. Only when you have achieved this unique situation will you feel happy about making regular return calls. And not until this friendly relationship exists will your customer be happy about welcoming you back to his office, warehouse or store.

So, let us now discuss how we can achieve this positive and friendly buying situation. And then have it work to your advantage.

Be Punctual

The first tip is simple. *Be punctual.* If you have made an appointment, don't you dare be late. You may well have a genuine excuse for not being on time, but the buyer will not be interested. He is a busy man and the last thing he wants to do is hang around waiting for some stupid salesman to turn up. If you can't be punctual, don't make appointments. It's far better to turn up cold than to get the buyer in a bad or negative mood just because you got stuck in the traffic. However if you really do have to break an appointment, simply phone him and explain. In plenty of time. Never, ever, leave him in the lurch.

Use a firm handshake
That gets you off to a good start in developing a good impression.

Smile
You must learn to SMILE. Your smile can be infectious and when used properly it can also be quite devastating. Just try smiling at complete strangers and see what happens. Usually they will smile back. And another thing, you just try

being angry or even indifferent towards someone who is smiling at you. It's very difficult isn't it? So, smile, gets your buyer smiling back, and he is well on his way to being on your side.

Remember his Name

Your first lesson is this. Remember your buyer's name. Like most of us he will undoubtedly consider his name to be amongst his most important possessions, and there is nothing that is more likely to irritate a buyer than to hear his name mispronounced or, even worse, ignored. So learn his name, get it right, and *remember to use it*. And by this I mean, from an early stage use the name that he prefers you to use. It has become increasingly fashionable for a salesman to use first names in a selling environment. If he has no objections and that's the way he likes it – fine, but if he is still formal enough to prefer you to use the 'Mr.' word, then do so. By all means try your hardest to get on first name terms quickly: it will help your relationship dramatically, but if your buyer really does object to this modern day familiarity, then respect his wishes. He is the boss and you cannot afford to annoy him. Not if you want his business.

Be Sincere
Be sincere at all times, you cannot fake friendliness.

Collect Information

Next you will have to consolidate the initial friendship you have already developed by entering into an even closer business relationship. To help you in this objective you will need to collect and then maintain various pieces of information of a more personal nature, and, to make sure that they are remembered, write everything down on your Account Card.
Imagine this scene. During a call your buyer tells you that next day he is taking his wife to the theatre. As soon as you leave, simply make a note on your Account Card and then on your next call you will be in a position to ask him about his evening out. He may well be impressed that you have remembered, but almost certainly he will be pleased that you have cared enough to ask. He will further realise, even if only subconsciously, that, if you care enough about his personal life, you are also likely to care about his business. And that's certainly a whole lot better than having him think that all you care about is how large the order is. Don't you think?

Well, now you are on your way to cultivating that important friendly relationship.

So far so good.
Let us now take a minute to summarise the situation so far.
To create a friendly atmosphere we must:-

- Be Punctual
- Use a firm handshake
- Smile
- Remember the buyer's name
- Be Sincere
- Collect information

But there's more.

We have now discussed various techniques that will help you to achieve that important friendly relationship. It is now in order for me to give you some words of warning. Don't get carried away, beware of creating too great an intimacy with your buyer. With everyone you meet in life you will find that there is a boundary over which you should never cross. Customers are no different. Never forget, and at the same time, never let your customer forget, that the sole reason for you being with him today is *to do business, and that you are primarily there for his order.* You will find that you can easily avoid any such problems if you simple cross-check that you are observing all the normal courtesies. Use those little words like "Good Morning" and "Thank You". They still have a place, and they still work. Believe me.

Here is another important, but obvious tip. Avoid, at all costs, discussions of a controversial nature. He may have a "hobby horse", and he may well like to sound off about all and sundry. Get him moaning or attempting to put the world to rights, and you may well find it difficult, if not entirely impossible, to get him back into a sensible buying mood. In short the best advice in this situation is to avoid any topic of conversation that could possibly have negative overtones.

Next comes what I would describe as one of the basic commandments of selling that must be totally obeyed at all times. It is this. *Always avoid any temptation whatsoever to criticise your competitor or the competitor's products.* Never be tempted to do so, as all the buyer will hear is adverse criticism about his own past buying habits. Even if the customer himself passes uncomplimentary remarks about the competition, you must resist any opportunity to agree or gloat, or you will find yourself falling into a simple trap. It's almost impossible to comment adversely on any aspect of the competition's activities without some of that criticism being reflected back onto the buyer. So don't do it. Ever.

I have now outlined some of the major steps that will help in developing a friendly relationship with your buyer. You may well be able to add to the points we have already discussed, but the really important point to remember is that without developing a friendly atmosphere you are just not going to get started. No matter how good your sales presentation may be.

So, remember. To create a friendly atmosphere you must:-
- *Be punctual*
- *Use a firm handshake*
- *Smile*
- *Use your customer's name*
- *Be sincere*
- *Remember personal details*
- *Be polite*
- *Do not get too friendly, but stay businesslike*
- *Never criticise the competition*

2) Increase the buyer's self regard

After you have created a friendly atmosphere the next stage in the "selling yourself" programme is crucial, as it helps to generate, in the buyer's mind at least, a desire to listen to what you really have to say. We call it increasing the buyers self regard or esteem. There are a number of ways in which you can increase the customer's self esteem, and we will now discuss just a few of them.

Be Complimentary
Firstly, try passing a few genuine and sincere compliments. Note that I said 'sincere.' For example you can be complementary about such things as the window display, or the shop's layout, especially when the displays have been prepared by the buyer himself. No doubt he would have taken a great deal of time and trouble over them, and you will benefit if he gets a feeling of pride on hearing constructive comments from you.

Whose idea was that?
There is no reason why you should not endeavour to allow the customer to think that your ideas were his. This is not all that easy but with some finesse it can be achieved. Everyone likes to think that they have good ideas, and if you can get the buyer to accept one of your ideas as his own, then be gracious and listen to what he has to say.

Listen
The ability to listen does not come easy to any of us, especially to those who feel that they have the 'gift of the gab'. Most salespeople talk too much. It turns buyers off. You must be just as prepared to listen and that means really listening - without any interruption.

Warning
A word of warning is in order here. While attempting to increase the buyer's self

esteem you will make every effort to avoid any obvious insincerity and soft soap. And you must never, ever, argue or talk down to a buyer. Insult your customer, or get his back up, and you will fail in your objective to increase your buyer's self esteem.

You have so little time
Having said that, it is also in order for me to highlight the fact that you will probably have a maximum of just one minute in which to create this friendly atmosphere and increase the buyer's self esteem. But with practice, the true professional can easily accomplish this task in a few opening seconds, with a few well chosen words and with positive action.
To sum up

- *You will pay sincere compliments*
- *You will listen –without interruption.*

By now you have learned how to create a friendly atmosphere and how to increase the buyer's self esteem. Your next step is to gain the buyer's confidence.

3) Gaining the buyer's confidence
The next important point is to gain the buyer's confidence. This means that your sole aim is to get him on your side and thinking along the same lines as you.
The simple truth is that buyers will not place orders unless they are confident that they will not regret it later. So, in everything that you say and do you must work towards your objective of gaining the buyers confidence in you, in your product and with your company.

Call regularly
Having sold the customer once, your job is now to follow through and continue to make regular repeat calls. Regularity is the key. Not necessarily frequently, but always regularly, and you and only you will have to decide just how often each follow-up call should be made. Whether a call justifies a fortnightly, a monthly or an eight-weekly visit, it's your decision. But what you must do is call on a regular basis, so regularly in fact that, even without an appointment system, your customer will gradually begin to get some idea as to when you will next be around.
Reliability breeds confidence, and confidence generates business. **Always.**

Demonstrate that you understand his business
To begin with, you will find it extremely helpful if you can demonstrate, that all flannel aside, you totally understand and appreciate the type of problems he is likely to have. You can also show him that you really do have some genuine

knowledge of wholesaling and/or retailing. You should be able to come to grips with such subjects as stock levels, stock turns, mark-ups and discounts. You will have gained his confidence whenever he feels that he can discuss his business with you on an equal and intelligent level.

And Help him
One of the best tips I can give you is to make suggestions that will be helpful to your buyer. As you travel around your area, you will be visiting many various and variable stores. You will not help noticing how other successful traders do what is right and profitable. This wealth of experience should enable you to diplomatically suggest ways in which his business might be improved. For example, you might come up with a new concept in merchandising; you might even point out to him that by siting his till in a different position he could generate extra benefits by exposing his customers to a wider range of impulse sales. I am sure that you can suggest other methods of making his business more successful and profitable.

All this will help you to gain your buyer's confidence. Then having gained that confidence you must make every effort to maintain and strengthen it. And whilst we are talking about confidence there is one fast and sure way of losing it. So it is vital that you:-

Keep your promise
Remember this – *it never pays to make a promise that you cannot keep.* For example you may have every reason to think that you or your company can make a particular delivery date, but before you start to make any promise – check. It is always preferable to say that you will do your best rather that to make a firm promise that you cannot personally guarantee.

Another point to remember is that no matter how efficient you are there will come a time when something does go wrong. It may genuinely not be your fault; someone in the warehouse or accounts department may mess things up for you. At times like this the professional salesman will handle all complaints quickly, while efficiently maintaining the credibility of both the company and the buyer. The confidence of the customer is then maintained and the friendly relationship stays intact.

All these ideas may seem obvious at first, but you will not want to take the chance of overlooking any of them.

And here is yet another step that you must take if you are to maintain your buyer's confidence.

Resist overselling.
You must always resist overselling, or overstocking. There is probably nothing

that is more likely to shake a buyer's confidence than by overstocking, or by delivering merchandise that he did not actually order. You must ensure that he gets exactly what he ordered, and, this is even more important, make sure that he knows exactly what he has ordered.

I will go even further.
You should never be tempted to allow your customer to order more than you know he will actually require. If he orders in the correct quantities to meet current consumer demands you can soon go back for those repeat sales. Get the ordering right and you will have the customer's confidence. Get it wrong and you will lose it.

Furthermore, if you can gain the buyer's trust and there is a real bonus in it for you.

The bonus is that you are now one step nearer to achieving another important objective for every salesman. And the bonus?

By taking the ordering out of the hands of the buyer you will sell more.

With your knowledge of the consumer demand that there is for your product you should be in a better position than your buyer to see that he is stocking all the products in the right colours and sizes and in the correct quantities.

And you will know that you have succeeded in obtaining the buyer's confidence when:-

The buyer asks you to make up his order for him.

Any customer that allows you to make out an order is demonstrating trust. *Never abuse that trust.* If you do, and you subsequently lose that trust, it is likely that you will find it difficult to retrieve it. When the salesman is trusted, his Company is trusted. You therefore have a huge responsibility to see that your Company can justify every claim that you personally make for it.

Let's revise the methods of gaining a buyer's confidence. Remember that in order to gain the buyer's confidence you must

- Demonstrate that you understand his business.
- Be helpful
- Keep your promises
- Call regularly
- Resist overselling

And your ultimate objective is to gain the buyer's confidence enough to take the ordering out of his hands. And put them in yours.

4) Show your Enthusiasm
You should always be enthusiastic, and that enthusiasm must clearly show through. Just remember how excited you were when you first saw that new product. Retain that enthusiasm, it can be highly contagious and it will always rub off on your buyer. Be genuinely enthusiastic about every single product in your line, and more importantly, cultivate enthusiasm for what those products will do for your customer. Enthusiasm, when it is not overdone, is one of the most important assets that a salesperson can possibly cultivate.

William McFee in his book "Casuals of the Sea" said "The world belongs to the enthusiast who keeps his cool," This is first rate advice for every salesman. And if you can't be enthusiastic about your products, how can you possibly expect the buyer to be.

Summary
Having discussed the type of atmosphere that needs to be present during a sales call, and also the ideal relationship that has to exist between your self and the customer, we can now go on to build your sales presentation. But before we move on to the next Chapter I want to repeat something for extra effect.

A sale is only likely to result when the "total selling environment" is favourable. So let us just go over, once more, the four basic rules that a salesman needs to follow to achieve this ideal selling situation. You will need to

> **1) Cultivate a friendly relationship**
> **2) Increase the buyer's self esteem**
> **3) Gain the buyer's confidence**
> **4) Show your enthusiasm**

Go back over these points, go over them carefully, and rehearse them until your attitude and behaviour automatically reflects everything that you have learnt. Then, and only then will you be ready to start building that sales presentation. And remember a sales presentation, however professional, is doomed to failure unless the total selling environment is favourable.

Here is one final question for you. *"When is the **best time** to get an order?"*

Have you thought about it? "What's you answer"

Well, the correct answer is - **When you have just written an order.**

The reason is that after a successful call you will be feeling good and your enthusiasm will be high. That's the right attitude to have before make your next call.

One Further Tip

It always pays to hand out a professional business card every time you see a customer or a prospective customer. It reminds him of who you are and what you are selling.

CHAPTER 4

BUILDING YOUR SALES PRESENTATION

You will now be provided with the tools that will enable you to design a professional, yet very personal, sales presentation for every single individual customer. But remember, unless you know precisely what you are doing, and why you are doing it, you will flounder and act like an amateur. If your sales presentation, or sales pitch as it is sometimes called, does not follow these vital guidelines you could even end up losing the order. On the other hand by being fully aware of what you are doing, and knowing why you are doing it, you will act in a polished and competent manner. The good salesman not only knows that a certain technique works, but he knows **why** it works.

We will now discuss what works and why.

The Sales Presentation
The ideal sales presentation is made up of a number of separate and unique components that, welded together in the right sequence, will be devastating.
Here are the six basic rules that, if followed, are guaranteed to make your sales presentation win you bigger and better orders.

1. *Acquire product knowledge*
2. *Use sales aides*
3. *Use a set selling pattern*
4. *Anticipate objections*
5. *Make it easy to decide*
6. *Ask for the order*

1) Product Knowledge.
You will never deserve to write an order unless you have a complete understanding of what your product is; what it does; how much it costs; what benefits it will bring, and the PROFITS it will generate for your customer. You will notice that I said "deserve" and I mean it. From time to time you may strike lucky, you may just pick up the occasional easy order, but that's not selling, and you will really not deserve business that you get that way. You will find that there are plenty of "order takers" in the world of consumer products. They will always be there and they will scrape a living. This is particularly true when orders are being taken for high turnover, well advertised, consumer demand products. Order takers have their place, but they can never ever expect to receive any form of real advancement whether it is remuneration or promotion.

You, on the other hand, will succeed in achieving your ambitions and

objectives. *You are going to stand out from the crowd and shine.*
So, once you have familiarised yourself with what it is you are **really** selling, and you have developed all the product knowledge on every item in your range, you have now become an expert on each and every product. There is no question about it. The person who is weak on the finer points of salesmanship, but strong on product knowledge will outsell any sales person who has not done their homework.

And there is no excuse for not demonstrating that all important product knowledge. All the information you will need is there and readily available for the asking. It is in the company literature. It's on the product label or pack. Read it and assimilate all the salient and technical points that will make you a real expert on every single product in your line.

The most important thing that has to be mentioned here is that every single product has what is called a U.S.P. – a "unique selling point".

The U.S.P. is that one, or more, aspect of a product which makes it stand out from the competition. It is the component that makes the product totally special, different or unique.

It may well be the overall quality of the product; it may be the item is new, or it has some other special or unique feature; it may even be the profit or the price. But whatever it is, every product will have at least one feature that is unique and that sets it apart from other apparently similar products.

As full product knowledge will also assist you in gaining the buyer's confidence, there is simply no excuse for not having a complete knowledge of your products or services. You owe it to yourself. You owe it to your Company. You owe it to your customer.

And another important tip. It will not do any harm to familiarise yourself with some knowledge of the competitors line. It may well help you overcome some objections.

2) Use Sales Aids
Sales aids are so important to every good presentation. Sales aids brighten up a presentation and stop it from becoming dull.

Whether you are supplied with leaflets, photographs, price lists or simply a sample of the product, your sales aids are there to be used. **So use them.**
You can use almost anything from a pencil to a piece of string but let us discuss some examples of items that are regularly used as selling aids.

Samples
Product samples are very precious and must be handled and presented with the utmost care. Whatever the product, your sample must be treated with the

importance it deserves. If the merchandise is important to you and to the buyer then your sample of the merchandise must be treated with equal care and respect.

A sample shows the buyer exactly what he will be getting, and can even be used to demonstrate how the product will look on his shelf. In fact, samples should be used to highlight every presentation. Another important point to bear in mind is that a damaged, crumpled or worn out sample reflects badly on you, your company, and more importantly on the product itself. You have no further use for a less than perfect sample. *Throw it away, and replace it.*

Whilst on the subject of samples, let me give you one further piece of advice.

At all costs try to avoid leaving a sample with a prospective customer. If you ever fail to convince him with your story and he asks you to leave a sample so he can think about it – don't do it. Politely explain that this is the only sample you have, but you would be more than willing to arrange for some literature on the product to be sent on to him. If you leave a sample with him I can guarantee that as soon as you have left him he will forget all about it and it will be left in his office or showroom where it will sit gathering dust with all the samples that others have left.

Experience shows that the practice of leaving samples is one that invariably has a zero chance of success.

Literature, Leaflets and Brochures
Use all the literature that you are provided with, and keep yourself up to date with everything that is published about your company or its products. And here is a further thought. If you cannot be bothered to read the literature, you can hardly expect someone else to. So do your homework. Using product leaflets in your sales presentation is one thing. Handing out leaflets to your buyer is quite another. Unless the handing over of literature actually forms an integral part of your presentation do not give anything to the buyer until you have had your say. That is until after you have finished your presentation. You will then avoid any distraction of him reading a brochure when he should actually be listening to you. Unless you can keep his full attention you may well lose him. And rightly so.

Plan Slips
One of the simplest, and certainly one of the most effective sales aides, is the Plan Slip. Simply take a blank piece of paper and jot down all the important points as you develop your sales arguments and include the entire product benefits (U.S.P.) as they arise during your talk. Write all the benefits on the plan slip in the order that you recommend them and finally underline the profit that the buyer is likely to make from the deal.

Your Brief Case
Your brief case is a sales aid. It tells the customer a lot about you. A clean, tidy brief case is the sign of a tidy mind. Keep it that way.

The Video Presentation
If you have been provided with any form of visual or computer aid don't leave it in the car. It is a professional and expensive tool. So keep it with you – it is designed to do all the selling for you, and anything that makes your life easier must be used with enthusiasm.

Summary
Remember that all sales aids will work for you if you let them. You have no excuse for not including at least one of these proven sales aids in your presentation. So do it. Your sales will benefit in a most dramatic fashion.

3) Use a Set Selling Pattern
I believe that to be successful you must develop a set selling pattern. And I am not talking about learning a speech or a script "Parrot Fashion".
Totally programmed, pre-rehearsed presentations may have their place in selling but as far as the retail salesman is concerned they have a number of inherent problems. In particular the set speech can never be tailor-made to suit each and every individual customer. Worse, an inexperienced salesman can be reduced to helplessness whenever he comes across a new or unforeseen objection and he can flounder whenever the conversation gets steered into a direction that was not previously considered at the rehearsal.

When I talk about using a set selling pattern this is what I mean.

Whatever the style of your sales presentation, you must adopt the right attitude. You are going to keep control of the discussion. You will always ask the right questions, and you will never allow yourself to speak in a haphazard way about any of your products.

In using a set selling pattern you will always remember that, as every buyer is different, every presentation must be custom built for that single individual person. You will then avoid the pitfall of having your presentation sound as if it is a set speech that has been learnt in a classroom. Rather it will appear, and sound like, the truly professional business discussion that your presentation really is.

The most popular, and without doubt, the most highly effective method of maintaining a set selling pattern is to base your presentation on the tried and tested AIDA formula.

AIDA = ATTENTION – INTEREST- DESIRE – ACTION

Let us discuss each of these points further

ATTENTION
Gaining the buyer's attention. This includes the cultivation of the friendly atmosphere through the friendly greeting, the passing of sincere compliments and the gaining of the buyer's confidence. But, more importantly, it also means getting the buyer's attention, perhaps by showing him something interesting, different or NEW.

INTEREST
You have to get your buyer interested in what you have to say. You will therefore need to establish his buying motives. In other words, why does he want to buy? You will need to get him totally involved in your presentation.

DESIRE
You must now generate a real desire in the mind of the buyer to want to stock your products. Now, and only now, can you sell the product benefits and support those product benefits by highlighting the unique features of the item to be sold.

ACTION
Ask for the order

In other words – Close the Sale.

But before we move on, let us just review those important aspects of building a sales presentation that we have discussed so far.

- *Know your product*
- *Use your Sales Aids*
- *Use a set selling pattern.*

We are now ready to move on to what is one of the most important aspects of salesmanship.

4) Anticipating Objections
An objection is any reason that is given for not buying. As a professional salesman you will learn how to anticipate objections and answer them before they are asked. Experience is going to teach you the sort of objections that your

buyer is likely to bring up. But don't worry too much about that now. Later, a full chapter is devoted to showing you how to overcome objections. In the meantime please bear in mind that objections will always occur and you must be ready to face them head on.

5) Make it Easy to Decide

What do I mean? Well, you should make it easy for the buyer to come to a quick decision on a point that you have raised. You will be sure to avoid asking any questions that will force your buyer into answering in the negative. In other words you will give him the choice of two alternatives – both of which are equally advantageous to you. For example "Do you want the blue or the green?"

6) Ask for the Order

In selling we must accept that "asking for the order" is a vital, if not the major aspect to using a set selling pattern. In any realistic selling situation, asking for the order – in other words closing the sale – is the final moment of truth. When I speak about "asking for the order" I find that I am often faced with probably the one statement that the newcomer to sales will find the most obvious. Yet this is the one aspect of selling that they are most likely to have trouble with. Indeed I am always surprised, especially when I happen to be at the receiving end of a sales presentation, to witness a salesperson who, having got the patter off perfectly; having demonstrated the product well; having then really got me really interested in the product; then forgets to ask for the order. If I am wrong, and the salesman did not actually forget, then the only excuse that I can possibly make for him is that he was so frightened of getting a "NO" that he ignored or overlooked the close.

But why should this be?

The buyer is there to buy is he not? You are there to sell are you not? This then is an indisputable fact. You must therefore get used to asking only positive questions and you must certainly never give the buyer the opportunity to answer in a negative way. This is a serious business situation, not a social gathering, and you are there and are paid to generate sales. Your buyer needs merchandise. He needs to buy before he can sell. If he does not buy the goods from you he will certainly buy elsewhere. Remember that you will often be doing the buyer a favour if you simply – *ask for the order. Simply*

SUMMARY

We have now discussed what is, in essence, the Salesman's Code of Practice. The 4 rules that will help you create a favourable selling situation together with your 6 rules for building a successful sales presentation. These 10 rules add up to total success in selling. They are, in effect, a salesman's 10 commandments. Learn them. Understand them. Use them.

Be aware of them and let them take you along the path of true professionalism in selling.

To create the ideal selling environment, and to build the ideal sales presentation you will need to

1) CULTIVATE A FRIENDLY ATMOSPHERE
2) INCREASE THE BUYER'S SELF ESTEEM
3) GAIN THE BUYER'S CONFIDENCE
4) SHOW YOUR ENTHUSIASM
5) KNOW YOUR PRODUCTS
6) USE YOUR SALES AIDES
7) USE A SET SELLING PATTERN (AIDA)
8) ANTICIPATE OBJECTIONS
9) MAKE IT EASY TO DECIDE
10) ASK FOR THE ORDER.

In the next chapter we will discuss selling techniques, including how to close a sale, in greater depth, but before we do I want to give you one further tip.

YOU HAVE GOT TO BELIEVE

- You have got to believe that you are a great salesman.
- You have got to believe that your Company is an honourable one.
- You have got to have the confidence to believe that your products are the best in the field.
- You have got to believe that those products are worthy of your customer and that they will generate greater profits and prestige for him.
- You have got to have faith in yourself.
- You have to believe in the power of positive thinking

In short –

YOU HAVE GOT TO BELIEVE

CHAPTER 5

THE PRE-PRESENTATION CHECK-LIST

There is only one thing more important than your sales presentation, and *that's the homework you do beforehand.*

I hope that we have already agreed that every sales call is different, and that no two buyers are alike. So, be prepared – you are a professional and you just cannot afford to leave anything to chance.

Every aspect of your sales presentation must therefore be carefully checked out, planned and rehearsed. *Again and again.*

Then your chances of success will improve dramatically. You will be ahead of the game and leagues ahead of your competition. And that is just where you want to be.

However, before your own personal take-off, you will need to go through this complete check-list in very much the same way that an airline pilot will check out his machine and his instruments before he requests permission to taxi down the runway.

The whole of your sales presentation will need to be checked over with just the same amount of precision and thoroughness until you are absolutely confident that you have finally perfected the most effective method that you could employ when dealing with each individual customer.

Remember, a buyer is someone with capabilities and limitations just like anyone else. In fact just like you. And he is someone who will need to be convinced that you have a good story to tell. So, your story must be right. It has to be both believable and interesting and you must be able to command his full attention. You know that really you are only going to get one crack at this presentation and so you just cannot afford to get anything wrong.

OK. Let us go through that fundamental, yet vital, check list in finer detail.

Most of the background information that you are ever likely to need should already be recorded on the customer's account card but it must include.

- *Try to remember names*
  First of all you should remind yourself not only as to the buyer's name, but also the names of any of his staff that you are likely to make contact with. Every employee in the buyer's store could be helpful to you in various ways. They are responsible for receiving stock, getting the stock out onto the shelves, and, more importantly, recommending products to the consumer. Every member of the store staff can help with moving

your product on. That is why you must learn their names and develop a friendly relationship with everyone. You will ignore your customer's staff at your peril.

- *Is this the right buyer*
  You will double check that the person you are seeing is actually the person that you can negotiate with and that he is the person that can actually make the final buying decision. As a salesman you will never be unduly overawed by someone in authority so from the outset you will aim at getting in to see the man at the top. The reason for this is simple. The more authority your negotiating partner has, then the better your chance of ultimate success.

- *What type of customer is he?*
  The notes in your records will jog your memory as to what type of customer he actually is. Is he a retailer, wholesaler, market trader, distributor? And perhaps what is even more important is for you to know what type of business he actually *thinks* he has.

- *What is his main buying motive?*
  The next thing that you will need to know is this. What actually makes him tick from a business point of view? Why would he buy from you? In other words, what are his buying motives? You must understand that, although every buyer obviously has a constant need to buy merchandise in order to stay in business, the chances are that he will be motivated into a buying situation by one or more reasons.

So now we can move on to discuss buying motives in greater depth.

CHAPTER 6

BUYING MOTIVES

A 'buying motive' is the reason why someone purchases something. These buying motives apply to all of us whether we are buying for business purposes or simply for our own personal needs or pleasure. Such facts of life will apply equally to yourself as well as your buyer. We all make purchases for a number of different reasons.

But what is more important to you as a salesperson, is to know **why** that buyer will give you an order, or more specifically, why he would buy that certain something from you.

You need to remember that there are a number of reasons why a person is likely to be motivated into buying. Therefore you must quickly establish what your customer's **actual** buying motive is. If you get it wrong you may easily lose the sale and deserve to.

If you want to sell from strength it is important that, from the very start, you set out on the right track.

To explain 'reasons for buying' in more detail let us look at some of the major buying motives and learn how they can be identified, and then used to exploit the selling situation to your best advantage. These then are the 6 major reasons why anyone will buy anything.

1) Price

Today, there are an ever increasing number of superstores, discount houses, bargain basement, pound stores and the like, who, through enormous bulk buying, are able to negotiate large discounts at source, and then pass these discounts on the public as price cutting promotions.

Do not be afraid of the big buyer. Selling the discount house is identical to selling any other normal retail outlet. The merchandise is the same, but in exchange for massive orders they will be looking for the appropriate discount or price reduction. But for such a deal to be profitable to you, your price is going to have to match the size of the orders.

Because of the "price cutting" war that has broken out everywhere you are likely to come across a number of smaller retailers who have convinced themselves that the only way to combat this type of competition is also to sell at very low prices.

There are retailers, and you will certainly came across them, who believe that the **only** way in which they can keep their customers is to always sell at the lowest possible price. Not only will they cut their profit margin to ribbons hoping that the customer will beat a path to the door, they will often concentrate on buying cheaper, bottom of the market merchandise. "My customers will not pay these prices" you will hear him bleat.

Selling junk lines and price cutting to a ridiculous level, unless it is restricted to a small selected range of loss leaders is the fast road to nowhere. Business graveyards are littered with such ventures.
There is no future for any trader who does not maintain his profit margins. Avoid these dealers like the plague. Unless, of course, you are in a position to profitably sell him that inexpensive, bottom of the range merchandise.

On the other hand there will always be a majority of retailers who need a constant supply of higher priced, high street items. These retailers are always on the lookout for new, quality or luxury products. One thing is certainly true. This type of buyer knows that his staff costs, his business expenses such as insurance and utility bills, and in fact all his direct overheads, are constantly rising. He is a realist and knows that he must maintain, if not improve, his trade margins. He fully realises the benefits that come from stocking a wide range of high ticket products. He knows that the more cash that goes into the till, the more gross profit he is going to make. This is the buyer who will succeed.

Stick with him and see that he gets what he wants – at the price that he wants.

I can give you one further tip on this subject. If ever you should find that you have reached an impasse on price, simply switch the conversation to quality, service and profit.

2) Profit

If Profit is the buyer's prime buying motive that is good news. And hopefully, that is why he is in business. So talk PROFIT. Total profit. This buyer will need to know all about trade margins, and how best those margins can be increased. He may want to talk about buying in quantity or even how to take advantage of promotional or special offers. You will tell him about settlement discounts, and you will sell him on all the regular, special and seasonal offers available. You will sell PROFIT. Profit per case, profit per item and basically you will talk about the amount of money going in his till.

3) Pride

If PRIDE is the name of the game, you will soon know it. From the outset you will get the very firm and distinct impression that this buyer takes enormous pride, not only in his store, but in the type of merchandise he stocks. You will find that over the years he has built up a reputation of a business that specialises in top quality, higher priced merchandise. He and his customers will therefore need the best quality available. And this is just what you are going to sell him.

You are going to convince him of the self-satisfaction that he will derive from stocking your products. You are going to sell "quality" and you will demonstrate that he should have every reason to be proud that he is stocking your products.

4) Greed

Sooner or later you will come across the greedy buyer. He will want to have his cake and eat it. Fortunately he is easy to spot. He may be looking for free gifts or something for nothing. He may well tell you that he will only buy from you when you have an extra bonus on the product. He will always try to squeeze you for an extra discount.

You, on the other hand, are going to have to stand your ground. You will explain that your Company's pricing policy is quite clear and fixed. Then you will point out that it would be grossly unfair to treat any single customer as a special case.

But really the best, and the only serious and practical way to deal with the greedy buyer, is to steer the conversation into a totally different direction, and make every attempt to get him thinking along more business-like lines. If you fail to move him on to an alternative buying motive you could well find yourself stepping on very dangerous ground. The greedy buyer will try to compromise you into making an unprofitable deal.

You however will not be shaken.

In the last resort however, if there really does have to be a final resort, you may well find that a premium or free gift might work with this buyer. This will be especially true when the buyer is not to be the actual owner of the business. However if a free gift has to be used as an incentive then make sure that, in return, you extract your pound of flesh.

There is no taste in nothing, and everything has to be paid for. And all premiums and free gifts must be paid for with extra business.

5) Fear

From time to time you will come across the buyer who, to a certain degree, is motivated by fear. For example, he may well fear that his competitor has an edge on him because he does not stock your product, although he is being asked for it. You must exploit this situation by encouraging him to fear that he is likely to lose customers if he does not carry your product line. Sometimes he might fear a price increase such as in a pre-budget period.

In all cases your job is simple. First you exploit his fear, then you reassure him, and then, finally, you take the order.

6) It solves a problem

You may well find that that the main reason your buyer wants to do business with you is that it will solve a problem for him. He might be having a problem with his current suppliers. They might not be able to produce the right goods at the right price. If you can offer him a service that is better than he gets from his present suppliers, whether it be in terms of delivery, availability, price, order size, colours or anything else:

Sell the benefits, **and take his order.**

CHAPTER 7

POLISHING YOUR PERFORMANCE

The final Pre-Presentation Check List

So now you know something about your customer and what his buying motives are. In other words you should now have a feeling for what turns him on - profit wise. But before we move on to the next stage, we should just stop for a second and ask a few basic questions and remind ourselves about

a) What actual reasons does your customer have for buying from you?

b) How often is he likely to buy?

The answers to these questions will give you a further mental profile of your buyer. This picture must be kept firmly in your mind while all the other components of your sales presentation are checked and double checked.

The next stage is to take another look at the customer's record card. This time you make a note of those products that he is already stocking and remind yourself that today you are going after those important repeat sales. Next you will check out those products that you intend to introduce him to on the next call. Then ask yourself a few further questions.

- *What about showing him a new line?*
- *What about demonstrating a special promotional product?*
- *What about offering a seasonal line?*
- *What about those products that are not currently being stocked?*

Check out all the opportunities that there are for a sale and refresh yourself with the U.S.P. for every product you are planning to present.

You will remember that your presentation will be further enhanced by the use of samples, brochures and literature.

You will then double check that everything you intend to take into the call with you is readily available and to hand. Check that you have all your samples, the literature, including price lists, and the sales aids that you are likely to need.

Remember – there is nothing worse than having to break off in the middle of your sales presentation to go back to the car for something you have forgotten. It's laziness, it's unprofessional and it's a sales killer.

Next, take a few seconds to check out your speaking voice. No, I am not suggesting that you immediately enrol for a course in elocution. Rather you should check that your sales story is likely to come across in a clear and precise manner.

And while we are on the subject of talking. Should ever find yourself suffering from one of those very annoying ticklish coughs – do something about it. There is a remedy awaiting you at every pharmacy.

One further tip on this subject.
I would always advise you to keep up to date with current affairs. If there is a radio in the car – keep it tuned to a local or news station. The worst that can happen is that you keep abreast of local traffic problems. At best you will be prepared to answer any questions on what is current news. You may even be able to supply the latest cricket score. That might be useful information to your buyer. And if the latest score is important to him it should be important to you.

Finally, you are going to run through in your mind the type of presentation that you will be making. Of course, it will be a tailored made presentation, and you will remember the ten sales commandments and all those points we discussed earlier. As you are planning on using a set selling pattern you know that it will be based on the AIDA formula. Remember

ATTENTION – INTEREST– DESIRE – ACTION

And you will be putting everything you have learned here into positive effect.

There is one further tip for you at this point. Your presentation will be much more interesting if you get the buyer involved in your discussion. The most reliable way of achieving this, and keeping him interested in what you are saying, is by asking questions.

Another easy way of involving him is to press home the product benefits and also incorporating a number of "You can's" into your presentation. A "You can" is a statement designed to personalise the product benefits by showing the buyer how he can be personally affected by the product.

Examples are:-

- *"You can stock the top brand"*
- *"You can increase your profits"*
- *"You can attract new customers*

But whatever sales presentation you have devised for your customer, and the winning presentation will obviously only come with experience, it is absolutely vital to adopt the correct attitude towards each and every single product in the line.

It is unfortunate, but perfectly understandable, that every salesman will have his own personal favourite product. The one single product that he likes above all others.

Perhaps the one that he feels more confident with, or the one that he is sure he can tell a good story about. A good salesman will not only sell his favourite product but will concentrate on selling the complete line with just the same confidence and enthusiasm.

Further, not only will he sell the full line, but he will give extra effort to those higher priced products or those items that generate the highest profit margin for his Company.

His own success depends also on the overall success of his Company. He who looks after his Company ultimately looks after himself.

CHAPTER 8

OBJECTIONS AND HOW TO OVERCOME THEM

What is an objection?

By now you should be totally familiar with your own 10 commandments. You will also now be aware that an important aspect of a successful sales presentation is developing the ability to anticipate and overcome objections from your buyer.

Whatever type of product or service you are selling, you should quickly acquire a second sense or some basic gut-instinct if you will, for every kind of objection or question that is likely to be raised by the buyer. Most objections can, and must, be anticipated by you, and then incorporated into your sales presentation. That way you can decisively overcome many of these objections or questions before they can cause you any serious damage.

On the other have we have to be realistic. We know that whatever we may actually say, or demonstrate, in our presentation, the likelihood is that the buyer may well have some doubts and will want to ask you some further questions that he will need an answer to. Simply, he might just want to know more about what exactly it is that you are offering him.

But before we go any further let me again define what is meant by an objection.

An objection is any reason that your customer has for not giving you an order.

You will quickly discover that objections can, in fact, come in all shapes and sizes. You will quickly realise that some objections are real. Some are imaginary. Some objections are genuine, and some are not. Some might appear merely as irritating little interruptions to your presentation, but occasionally your buyer may seriously be saying "NO". Sometimes he may be stalling for extra time to allow himself to think. He may be just asking a simple and straightforward question. But, that too could turn into an objection if not handled right.

You are a professional salesman and you are now going to learn everything you possibly can about objections.

But first let me underline this.

You must develop a second nature for recognising objections as soon as they come up, and cultivate the skills that will help you overcome them.

However there is good news. A genuine objection can, and often will, brighten up even the most dull and lifeless presentation, and for that reason alone, every objection should make a welcome contribution to a sales presentation.

So, from now on you will constantly be on the look-out for an objection but you will be especially vigilant during your final closing message.

When that objection does finally come up you can regard the situation as your own personal crossroads. Remember this;

There is nothing that you will ever learn about the art of salesmanship that is more important than dealing with objections.

So, be prepared and ready to meet your enemy head on. And anything that is so vital in selling that it can actually stand between you and your order must be discussed in great detail and at some length.

I want you to imagine that you are now well into the sales presentation and everything appears to be going along fine. Now, as I have already said, you must expect that at some stage, even with the most well rehearsed story, the buyer will start to ask you questions and may possibly even raise a question or two about your product or service.

The most important thing to remember at this crucial stage is that an objection is usually nothing more that a *"buying signal"*

I'll repeat that.

AN OBJECTION IS A BUYING SIGNAL

It is for this very special reason that you must never ignore a buying signal. Rather you should welcome every single objection. Apart from the mere excitement of accepting the challenge, I want you to realise that whenever a buyer raises an objection you can safely assume that he has already given some serious though and consideration to the points that you have raised so far. He may even have already made a mental picture of how he could use the product. He may even have already thought how best it could be displayed in his store. He may even have thought of a number of his regular customers that your new product will readily appeal to.

I want you right now to recognise a simple basic truth.

Whenever your buyer raises an objection all he is really saying to you is

"Convince me, I still need to be sold to"

Therefore I will repeat

EVERY OBJECTION IS A BUYING SIGNAL

So how do we handle these objections?

Before you can properly handle any objection you must first remind yourself of the customers buying motive just as we discussed in Chapter 6. Then you must ascertain whether or not the objection is a serious one or not. You have only one foolproof method of learning why the customer feels strongly about an issue and that is by discovering the degree of seriousness behind the objection.

It is vital that you pay very close attention to every single point raised by your buyer. Listen carefully and attentively. Never interrupt, and be absolutely sure that you hear the buyer out.

Be patient, bide your time, and before you answer the question, wait until you are sure he has finally finished with what he wants to say. Then, and only then will you be sure that you have heard the full objection. If you do not hear him out the chances are you will discover that, at best he will already have answered his own objection or, at worst, he will have given you the answer to the question that he really wants to hear. So listen – **carefully.**

However, let me add that if there is even the remotest of chances that you have not fully understood what his objection really is, ask him to repeat it, and this time *listen even more carefully.*

If you have carefully listened you should now be able to ascertain the true seriousness of the objection.

Once you are completely clear in your own mind what is the nature of the real objection is, you should answer his doubts quickly in a positive and constructive manner.

Then, as soon as you as sure that your explanation has been satisfactorily received, understood and accepted, you go directly back to where you were in your main presentation, and pick up from where you left off.

How do we answer Objections?
From the outset there is one useful tip that I would ask you to remember every time you reply to a buyer's question. And it is this.

Whenever possible try to turn the query round to your advantage. Say – *"I'm glad that you mentioned that, it's a very good point". "But, if you consider…………..".*
Then you must go on to describe a major factor of the product (U.S.P.) that is relevant to the question and the one that is most likely to appeal to your buyer. This response is a simple, but useful method that allows you to overcome an objection without the buyer fully realising it.
And here is another.

When a buyer throws an objection, try this suggestion, instead of responding with your usual stock answer, respond by posing a question back.

You can ask, *"Is that your only objection/reason/doubt/fear/problem?"*
The chances are that your customer will answer this question with either a positive "Yes" or a definite "No"

If he answers "Yes" then what he is really telling you is that he will buy if you are able to put him at ease and overcome, to his satisfaction, the one real doubt that he has for not giving you the order. You will now find yourself in a much stronger position so you can put all your weight into convincing him as to why he will be making a sound purchase. Then promptly ask for the order and close the sale.

Alternatively his answer to the question *"Is that you're your only objection"* may be *"No"*. In effect he is then giving you advance warning that there are further doubts at the back of his mind. Ask him to tell you about all the others. Listen, without interruption, and mentally collate all the information he may require if he is to react positively to your answers.

Be confident that you can now overcome all his objections in one fell swoop, and then you can smartly close the sale.

Here is another good tip that I think is always worth remembering. If you should ever start to experience any particular difficulties or if you ever find yourself getting bogged down, there is one sure way of quickly getting out of your dilemma.

Just ask the buyer to outline *"in three simple sentences"* his main objection to buying. From this information you can isolate his real objection and there you are, back in the game. You have now gleaned from him all the information you need, and you should be in a position to re-sell him from a much stronger position.

At this stage there is no harm in repeating that while you are overcoming his objections you must stay ever mindful of the importance of maintaining a friendly atmosphere, and of your need to protect the buyer's own self esteem. Never disagree with him, and most certainly never talk down to him. You must, at all times, understand his point of view, and demonstrate that you really understand his objections, whilst at the same time continuing to be polite, albeit firm and positive in your reply.

Some standard everyday objections.

We can now discuss in greater detail some of the various types of objection that you are likely to get, and we will learn how best you can deal with them.

But before we go any further I will say again ***"An objection is any reason that your customer has for not giving you an order"***. I will put it another way.

Whenever your buyer asks you a question - that is an objection.

If he queries something - that is an objection. If he says no – that is an objection.

In other words, whenever your buyer raises an objection he is simply saying

"You have not yet convinced me".

So let us now take a closer look at some of these potential problems and the opportunities that they can produce for you. Objections can occur

- *Before your presentation*
- *During your presentation*
- *After your presentation*

Pre-Presentation Objections
Make no mistake about it; objections can occur even before you get to make your sales presentation.

To start with the customer may refuse to see you. If he does, then that's an objection and it has to be dealt with. Alternatively you may find yourself in a situation where you will find it impossible to get beyond the secretary or receptionist.

There is another possibility. Your prospective buyer could be so busy telling you something of importance to him that he gives you little or no chance to get a word in or to get back into your presentation.

In reality there is only one successful method of overcoming any pre-presentation objection.

You must simply arouse his curiosity. You can make a short remark or statement, through his Secretary or Receptionist if necessary, that includes at least one important buzz word. **Profit** is a good buzz word. You can try telling him you have something **New** to show him. Or even something **unique or innovative.** Tell him something that will arouse his curiosity enough for him to want see you and listen to what you have to say. You will have to make the message short and snappy, and without actually telling him exactly what you have to offer, but you must arouse his interest to the level where he will have a real desire to know more.

In other words give his enquiring mind a going over and earnestly suggest to him that you have something that he cannot afford to ignore.

Get this right and few will be able to resist you. Curiosity killed the cat. It can kill this particular objection.

You can now go ahead with your presentation and then you can land the sale.

Objections during a presentation
A number of standard objections will arise in one shape or another every day. We will now discuss some of the most common objections that are likely to meet, and we will see how easy they are overcome them. You will come across them all the time.

"There is no demand for it."
Unfortunately a vast number of independent retailers still fall into the fatal trap of believing that they really know just what their customers want.

In fact they don't. Whatever they might tell you, retailers do not always know what their customers really want.

Daily, retailers will lose sales because they are not stocking the products that customers are actually asking for. Retailers have even been known to tell a customer "There is no demand round here for that product." I once had a retailer say to me "You are the tenth person that I have told this week. We have no demand for it. That product just does not sell in this neighbourhood." It's true, it really happened.

Therefore you must understand that the buyer is not necessarily the best judge of what products there will be a demand for. You must politely and firmly point out that you have full confidence that the product will sell in his store. Then you must demonstrate the benefits that he will gain by offering your product to his customers.

You can also pose the question "What particular product is there a good demand for in this area?" His answer may let you in with another selling point, or it might give you the reasons to sell another product in your range.

There is another objection very similar to "there is no demand for it", and it is this.

"We never get asked for this product."

The buyer may even go further and tell you that as a matter of policy he only stocks those products that are regularly asked for, but if he should ever get a request for your product then he will give further consideration to stocking it. But not until he is convinced that there is a genuine demand.

If that sounds like a valid objection, believe me, it is not. What is more it is very short-sighted. But you can't actually tell him that can you? You will just have to swallow your feelings and go right to the heart of the matter. Once again be polite; keep your cool; and explain that very often customers will not think to ask for a product which cannot be clearly and immediately seen on display. Therefore it really is a mistake to think that a product should not be stocked until it is asked for.

Another important point to make here is that sales in the retail trade are often made on impulse. And it is only by first spotting the product on display that a consumer can make an impulse purchase. How else would a consumer know that he has a need for that particular item? Just ask yourself how many times you have picked up a product in store because it was there. You certainly didn't go in for it, but on impulse you made a purchase. No impulse sale can ever be made on a product that isn't there.

There is yet another reason. Seeing a product on display will often jog a consumer's memory about a product that he has heard about, been recommended to, or seen advertised. Such a memory jog will, and frequently does, influence a retail sale.

Finally, you must press home the point that there can never be a sale from a product that is neither stocked nor displayed.

If he can't stock it, he cannot sell it. It's obvious but true.

"Sorry, I'm not interested."

This objection is often a ploy used to get rid of a fledgling salesman, especially when the buyer is busy or has no real inclination or motivation to hear what the salesman has to say.

Should you ever come up against this you will have to catch him unawares by throwing a question back at him? "You're not interested Mr. Buyer? Can you please tell me what it is that you are not interested in exactly?"

"I'm fully stocked"

On the surface it looks as if today is just not going to be your lucky day. He is fully stocked. There is nothing he needs, and he tells you so.
Don't you dare believe it?

Whenever you hear this, and you will, don't panic. Go straight into your friendly relationship routine and open up some two-way dialogue. Gain his confidence and gradually turn the subject towards business while trying to ascertain to your own satisfaction whether or not:-

- What he is saying is really true
- He is really fully stocked with <u>all</u> your products, or perhaps
- It is not really your products but rather your competitor's merchandise that he is actually overloaded with.

You can quite easily get to the truth of the matter by asking a series of searching questions or, if possible, by checking yourself to see just how much merchandise he really does have in his inventory. At the same time you can check to see just how long the goods have been in stock. If there is any doubt in your mind about either of these points, why not ask to see his latest delivery notes.

Should you ever be faced with a genuine overstocking situation it is your duty to discover why and how this happened. You can make some suggestions as to how you might give him some more support to move the stock out. You might suggest supporting an in-store promotion or some local advertising that will get the goods moving faster off the shelves.

Next ascertain whether all your goods are being correctly displayed and merchandised. Explain that better merchandising can, and will, dramatically improve his turnover and go on to suggest way of doing this. You can discuss indoor displays, offer promotional material, and suggest window displays. In short, show him, through your business like attitude that you are sincere and demonstrate by your ideas that you are genuinely interested in his problems and his business.

Be positive, and suggest that sales of your products should not stagnate but, on the contrary, will produce regular profits when the range is handled correctly within the store.

However if, on the other hand, you discover that the actual problem is that he really is fully stocked, but with products from one of your competitors, then you must stress the unique selling points (U.S.P.) of your products and respectfully explain, that rather than tie up cash in what is obviously dead stock, he would be well advised to give more support to your range of faster moving merchandise.

If, in spite of everything, you are still convinced that your customer is really holding sufficient stocks for his needs then it may still be possible to get an order.

You could close the sale on the basis of a later delivery date. Or perhaps on particularly favourable terms or even on the assumption that as prices are shortly to be raised he should order now to save money.

It's all worth a try – right. So, next time you meet "I'm fully stocked" you are not going to believe it until you have personally checked and explored all the possible alternatives.

"I am only interested if I can buy on sale or return".
This is another objection that you must never take too seriously. "Sale or return" or S.O.R. agreements are usually confined to mass merchandising products; magazines or newspapers. S.O.R. also referrers to those special self-service display units put up in a store that are regularly supervised by a merchandiser who will return at regular intervals to check, replenish and rotate the stock.

Your customer will know that most companies do not operate a "Sale or Return" policy.

If the buyer asks about S.O.R. he is really saying that he is not yet convinced that you have a product that will sell.

Once you realise this you should be able to dispel all his fears by going over the advertising and promotional activities that will be supporting the product. Prove to him that you do have confidence in the product, and that unless you truly believed that it would be possible for him to achieve a worthwhile amount of turnover, you would never have considered selling the product to him in the first place.

I will have to think about it".
Another great classic objection that the inept salesman could fall for. After all he didn't actually say "No" did he?

You will not be deterred however and you will use this objection to your own advantage.

The moment you hear *"I will have to think about it"* you will very quickly decide whether the buyer is simply procrastinating , or whether he really does want some extra time to carefully weigh up all the pros and cons that you have already put to him. Equally you must avoid creating an impression of being too anxious to close the sale.

After all, he may well have a genuine problem in that he personally finds it very difficult to make decisions. I said "may", and the way to make sure is to ask him.

"Is there any further information I can give you that will help you decide?"

He should then tell you, and the answer he gives is likely to contain his real objection to placing an order. If you have been listening closely you will know what the problem really is. Now you can close. Answer his objection and ask for the order.

"I will have to discuss it with my partner/boss etc."

This could well be a logical objection. Maybe he is not the actual buyer, or maybe he needs the approval of someone else before he can take on a new product. In these circumstances you must never allow him, if you can possibly avoid it, to give his version of your presentation to his partner or boss. Nobody can do that sales presentation better than you: he may well make a hash of it: you know more about the product, and you are better able to "sell" it. He most certainly can't, and he may well screw everything up, and you could well loose the sale. A more positive approach would be to ask him a simple question. When will your boss be available?" – Then suggest that you return later to make a further presentation to both of them. Make a firm appointment to come back later, and then make the presentation to the real decision maker directly.

"Your products don't move fast enough."

Now this can be a real challenge. Luckily, once again, it's not as bad as it initially it might seem. When you hear this you will first of all need to know

- *What the buyer really means when he tells you that your products are not moving fast enough,*

   and

- *How fast does he expect them to move? What was he actually expecting?*

As usual you will need to ask a number of searching questions, the answers to which will allow you to investigate the objection more deeply. If your buyer really does believe that there is some truth in his claim then you should immediately point out that your company has a wide range of products. The complete line aims to fulfil many and varies customer needs, and in fact the whole range should be looked at in total. Explain that, in your opinion, the range, when looked at overall, moves very quickly when compared with the competition.

However, if the line is genuinely sticking on the shelf then there is probably something wrong with the way the goods have been displayed or merchandised. You will need to check the situation for yourself and then make sure that the goods are displayed in the best possible location. If they are displayed correctly, then ascertain that they have been properly merchandised. You must, having gained that information, do everything possible to help your customer see the advantage of ensuring that every product is being merchandised to its absolute best advantage. Remember the old maxim – *if it can't be seen, it can't be sold.*

And another thing. Bad merchandising and dusty or damaged packs will always hinder sales. Keep the display clean and tidy.

Then, check that the appropriate show cards, posters, streamers or shelf-talkers are properly displayed. And what about sales leaflets? What about price lists and eye-stoppers? Analyse what exactly is being done within store to highlight the range of products to the consumer. If anything is wrong or missing, you must correct the situation urgently.

In-store promotions, window displays and good merchandising techniques must be openly discussed at frequent intervals with your buyer as all these activities can and will dramatically improve sales and get turnover moving a whole lot faster.

Perhaps you will now have found a genuine solution to his problem. By so doing you will demonstrate your own professionalism. You have overcome his objection. You can now take the order.

"I already have a large enough range."

This comment will be made in a variety of ways, and you are most likely to get it when you are trying to introduce a new line. Other ways that you might hear this objection can include

- *"My range is already large enough."*
- *"My customers already have a wide enough choice."*
- *"I stock everything that is required to satisfy my customer's needs."*
- *"Just check my range yourself. You will see that I have no need for any more lines."*

- *"It is just duplicating the lines I already carry."*

Basically your buyer is telling you that he has little or no room for any more lines. He may well have a point. Space is always at a premium, but your job is to convince him that there is likely to be a large and genuine demand for your products. And simply that's how this particular problem has to be tackled.

Firstly you will remind your customer that in today's business world, more than ever before, consumers demand a steady flow of fresh, new products, gadgets and ideas. Consumers have an insatiable appetite for anything new and are always on the lookout for the latest in style or fashion. Indeed they will often shop where they know they are most likely to find the most modern and up to date merchandise.

The word "NEW" has almost magical properties. Why else would it be constantly used in the advertising medium? "NEW" indicates up-to-date, modern: the latest. "NEW" projects a feeling in the mind of the consumer that he is dealing with a progressive and modern company.

It is important for you to realise that your buyer has to consider not only today's sales but his future business. A consumer that is forced to buy a new product from another store will very often go on to take all his future business there. Can your buyer afford to take that risk? **Ask him.**

You will also dramatically strengthen your argument if you point out that this new product complies with all the latest statutory regulations. Or, perhaps you can demonstrate that the product contains the very latest in technology. Perhaps this new product incorporates the latest in health and environmental issues.

In short, if there is any aspect of the product that is "NEW", then it is a U.S.P. Tell him about it. There is always another angle, isn't there?

Whether we like it or not and there are good arguments both for and against, we are living in a world of disposables. Whatever the economic situation today's consumer society always wants the latest model. Today's fashion. And it wants it now. Does your buyer really want to fall behind the times? Does he want to risk building a reputation for being old fashioned? **Ask him.**

Another useful point is that a new line can often fill a gap that exists in a particular product range. You must highlight this fact and point out that the greater the depth to a range then the higher the sales volume and the higher the profit that the range will generate.

Finally on this subject you can relate the new line to the back-up that the product will receive from advertising, public and press relations, and from all other consumer promotional activities. All promotional activities are designed to produce maximum sales. Not only for the product, but also for the buyer.

Do you think that your customer really wants to miss out on this exciting new opportunity? It is always your responsibility to see that both you and your buyer profits from something "NEW".

"Your product is too expensive."

Before you answer, remember that you must never allow the buyer to think that you believe the product to be too highly priced or even too expensive.

Having said that I also want you to remember that whenever you hear a comment that the price is too high, the chances are that the buyer has already decided that he needs the product, and he has probably already considered spending some of his working capital on the product. He does however need to be fully convinced that he is making a wise and sound investment.

You should remind him that in all walks of life there are always customers looking for an *up-market* or *quality* product. You can easily demonstrate, with the aid of a plan slip, the potential return on capital that he is likely to receive from such an investment. You can sell strongly on the net profit angle and also explain the advantages of offering a product with a higher unit sale. You can also point out that the extra initial cost of the stock is more than outweighed by the extra quality or by the extra profits that can accrue to him, and, if he is a wholesaler, to his retail customers?

This objection is closely linked to another that really means the same thing, but although said in a slightly different way, it is still designed to give you a headache – if you let it.

"Your price is too high for my market"

These will most likely crop up just at the same time as you are trying to introduce a new price list, or price increase. But the same comments will apply whenever price seems to be the main obstacle to buying.

A very common objection, especially during inflationary times, is the one that concerns price increases. And that is natural. No one likes to pay more.

Firstly though understand this. If the price increase is the true objection, it is important that you understand the reason for the price increase, and that you totally understand the reasons for it yourself. If you are in any doubt, go back to Head Office and get the information you need. After all you will need to know the truth if you are to handle the situation professionally.

Reasons may include increased raw material costs, or higher labour rates, but there may be others. Your Company might have a real need to improve on its own profit margins.

Whatever the reason, get all the available facts and be prepared.

It is absolutely vital that, when facing this problem, you let your customer fully understand that you are sympathetic towards him and that you genuinely know how he feels about suddenly being asked to pay more. After all, he is going to have to explain any price increases to his own customers.

Another important aspect to consider here is that whilst treating this objection in a totally positive manner, it is right that you avoid blaming the increase on any hidden forces. This way you will avoid arousing any suspicion on the part of your customer. Never go on the defensive when making your point, and continue to state your argument with factual comments.

I think that it is true to say that many salesmen feel slightly uneasy when dealing with price objections. Some salesmen are wary of even the most straightforward and genuine cost enquiry in case it leads to an objection on price.

The most important factor to remember is that price is not so much related to value, as much as it is related to what the buyer's perception is of what actually is "value for money."

You will therefore need to quickly establish the question of value in the mind of the buyer from the outset. When answering an objection that the price is too high you must then ask a number of pertinent questions, and the answers you get will help you to handle the original resistance to the price increase. If the actual objections is

"The price is too high"

- This is always one of the more difficult objections to overcome. My suggestion is that you can reply with one of the following questions:-
  "The price is too high? In what respect is the price too high?"
- "Please tell me, exactly what do you mean when you say the price is too high?"
- "Tell me, are you more interested in cheaper products or do you think your customer may be looking for quality."
- "Is there anything that you would recommend we could take out of the product to make
  it cheaper?

The answers you get will help you develop the most effective reply, and allow you to move on.

I will now give you a few other basic, but useful ideas on how to handle this particular objection.

The simplest way is to take your reply a stage further and if a price increase is actually his basic objection then there are a number of less direct ways of successfully dealing with it.

First of all compare your new prices with those of the competition. If your prices have had to rise you can be sure that market forces, especially as applied to labour and raw materials, etc., will mean that sooner or later, your competitor will also have to raise his prices – if he hasn't done so already.

You could also relate the price increase to the latest increase in the overall cost of living.

You might also emphasise how long it has been since the last price increase on that product. Constantly rising prices for just about everything have become so common place now that we are all inclined to accept increases as a matter of course. Even during periods of low inflation, utility bills, rent and other overheads continue to maintain their ever increasing upward rise

We may not like this concept of ever increasing prices, but we cannot help but accept it.

You should certainly point out that a higher unit sale price for the product will mean a higher cash profit in his till.

Let me finalise on this subject by reminding you that you must never show any uncertainty when replying to a customer's questions on price. And it must be repeated.

Avoid letting your customer gain the impression that you believe your prices are either too high, or that the product is too expensive.

If you don't believe that it represents value for money, why should your customer?

Objections after the Presentation

As soon as you have successfully answered the objection you should move on to the close, get the order and get out.

Never give the buyer to opportunity to say "that reminds me" as he brings up another point. Stay positive, change the subject if you have to, and make your next appointment, if you need to and move on to your next call.

OVERCOMING OBJECTIONS – LET'S SUM IT UP

There is no argument about it. Overcoming objections is an art. A skill even, but if you cannot develop these skills, if you don't enjoy the challenge; if you can't really cope with even the smallest objection; then, in my opinion, there is no place for you in selling, and the sooner you find yourself another career the happier you will be.

On the other hand, the salesman who enjoys this vital part of the selling game, and is excited by a determination to succeed will win through. He will write the order.

All the objections that we have previously discussed will come up time and time again. Keep a constant lookout for them, they may not always slap you in the face, they may be under the surface, but they will be there.

The objections we have discussed so far are only the major ones. There will be others.

So you must be constantly on your guard, be ready to anticipate and overcome them before any of them get the chance to raise their ugly heads.

I'll now repeat something that I said at the beginning of this chapter. I think it is important enough.

An objection is a buying signal. And in answering the objection you will make every effort to lead your customer into giving you that order and closing the sale.

CHAPTER 9

CLOSING THE SALE

Closing the sale is simply asking your customer for the order. And you will have to ask for the order before you can write it up on the order form. It's that simple. So what's the problem?

It has been said before but I will say it again at the outset.

If you cannot close a sale you cannot call yourself a salesman.

That's the simple truth. Don't be confused about it. The ability to "chat-up" a customer is absolutely no substitute for real selling. Closing is the moment of truth in every salesman's life. It sets him apart from the mere order takers and separates the men from the boys. In a most dramatic fashion.

After all, you have already made the effort to visit this customer, probably having already made a firm appointment to see the buyer. You have also made your personalised sales presentation.

So now you have to close the sale and leave with an order.

Yet there are still a large number of salespeople who seem to have a big problem with that part of selling that matters most. Closing the sale is the most hated part of selling, but what is there to be worried about?

Every experienced salesman knows that there are no hidden secrets in closing, but there are a number of basic principles that must be present in every closing situation if a sale is to be successfully made. There are principles and techniques that must learn and consciously applied to this vital part of your craft. Indeed closing is the area that needs the most attention in every selling situation.

Now - a word of warning. There are many successful ways of closing and there are all kinds of attitude that you might be tempted to adopt. But before we get into a full discussion on the types of close available to you, I want to say something on the subject of so-called *high pressure selling*. My advice – forget it. It really has no place in the world of FMCG selling.

High pressure selling will only antagonise your buyer and, as you will have to visit and revisit on a regular basis, you will need to maintain that friendly relationship. A successful close does not depend on high pressure and there should be no place for such conduct in your presentation.

Closing should be the easiest part of your job as a salesman. Don't be afraid to ask for the order. You have nothing to lose.

When to close?

In short – right from the beginning. Let me explain. From the very first moment you begin your presentation you must be prepared and ready to close that sale. With practice you will gradually develop an instinct for getting inside the buyer's mind and following his train of thought, but, in reality, this talent will take some time and only come with experience.

Meanwhile you will need to observe the buyer and train yourself to listen carefully to all his comments, questions and observations. You will then be able to assimilate this information and single out all those important "buying signals"

The question most frequently asked by trainee salesmen is

"But how do I know when the customer is ready to buy?"

If you are thinking in a positive manner you will see that the answer is straightforward and quite simple.

Your customer is ALWAYS ready to buy.

The point to underline here is that every buyer is there to buy. That's his job. He has to buy. Every buyer needs a constant supply of merchandise to keep his shelves fully stocked and his customers satisfied. Also understand that he will always be on the look-out for new or innovative products that will bring extra customers into his store and extra profits to his till. So buying is what he does. And selling is what you do.

Understand that you will never get his business until you close the sale, and you will readily see that what actually matters in closing is **knowing when to ask for the order.**

Remember that your customer has this continuous need to buy. So, stay positive.

Never think in terms of IF he will buy, but only WHEN he will buy.

In other words, always assume that your customer *will* buy, and you will realise how important it is to close the sale in a smooth, correct and professional manner.

So, when do you close exactly? To be honest, the main problem is that there is no fixed moment during any presentation when you will be definitely able to say to yourself **"This is where I close"**

You know that you will have to close sometime during the presentation consequently you will need to develop a sense of timing. Knowing *when* to close is something that comes naturally to some, but for most of us it takes some practice before it becomes instinctive.

How to close

You will remember, from a previous chapter, that you should consider every objection to be a "buying signal" and that your buyer will either consciously or subconsciously, be giving these "signals" as soon as he is ready to place an order. Let us take a look at some typical examples of what might well happen to you.

You are very close to landing the order and the customer is obviously considering how best he can use your product, and there are clear pointers to watch out for.

He may, for example, suddenly demonstrate a more enthusiastic attitude towards you and the product. He might even indicate his agreement with points that you are making by nodding his head or giving you other signals of approval. He may well pick the product up and examine it. He may also give you a verbal sign that he is ready to buy.

He might well ask some pertinent questions. Questions like *"When can you deliver?"* Or perhaps *"How well is it selling?"*

These and questions like them will indicate that he is already sold. Answer the question and then take the order.

It's so important that we shall go over this particular point once again.

As soon as you have spotted the buying signal there is only one course of action to take. Close the sale.

When you incorporate one or more of the following proven closes into your presentation and will surely follow.

The Order Form Close

By far the simplest, and certainly the quickest, way to close a sale is to use the order form close. You bring out your order form, as early in the presentation as realistic, and place it in front of you in full view of the buyer. This way your buyer knows that you are in earnest and ready to do the business. All you need do at the right moment is to ask for the information you require to complete the order form. Ask the appropriate questions as you progress with the presentation.

- *"What's the delivery address?"*
- *"Do you want the blue or the green?"*

If the order requires the customer's signature, you fill in the order then turn it round and ask him to 'OK' it.

Now here is a good tip. Never ask him to *sign* anything. *Signing* a document is a serious matter, and it may give him something to worry about. But there is nothing sinister about being asked to 'OK' something, is there?

Once the form has been OK'd you have closed. You have the order.

The Puppy Dog Close

This is a great close and it works well for many consumer products. Called the 'puppy dog close' because this is how puppies are sold. A puppy is put into the arms of a potential customer and then the smart salesman just sits back and waits. You could learn something from this. Get your buyer to hold the product, allow him to play with it, touch it, and feel it. Let him imagine what would happen if he didn't stock this item. Get him to the stage where he likes it so much that there is no way in which he is going to give it back. He is sold. Close the sale.

The Balance Sheet Close

I am now going to discuss what is usually called the balance sheet close, or the Summary List Close.

It is claimed that the great Sir Winston Churchill would often use this system whenever he needed some help with solving a particular problem. It is a good plan that works in everyday life, and it will work for you.

Now, whenever you ever feel that a buyer is having some difficulty in making up his mind you could suggest that he takes a leaf about of Churchill's book.

Take a sheet of blank paper and draw a line straight down the middle from the top to the bottom. You now have two columns. On the top of the right hand column you write 'NO' and on the left side you write 'YES'

Next, explain that whenever Sir Winston found himself stuck with a problem he would list all the reasons for saying 'Yes' followed by all the reasons for saying 'No'. Then he would make his final decision by comparing the two columns and would choose to go with the side that contained the highest number of reasons.

What you do now is start to write. In the 'Yes' column you list all those reasons why your customer should buy. You will list all the product benefits. All the USP's. All the 'yes's.' The profit margins. You will itemise every single thing that the product has in its favour.

A good salesman, who knows his product, should be able to list well over a dozen, but the more you add the better.

Now comes the clever part. You now turn the piece of paper around and suggest that you buyer lists all the reasons that he has for not buying. The, and this is important – you shut up, and give him no help whatsoever.

I must repeat that you *shut up*. You leave him to it.

My guess is that without any help from you, he will find it impossible to list more than four objections. You then compare the two lists and you have him. **You close the sale.**

The Alternate Close

A popular and often a most devastating close is the 'Alternate Close' Put simply all you have to do is offer the buyer a choice between two situations, both of which are equally favourable to you.

Remember – make it easy to decide.

Here are some suggestions of typical questions that, when asked correctly, can be used to decisively bring the issue to a head, and will determine whether or not the buyer is ready to decide.

You can ask *"Which location in your store would best suit a display of these products?"* Then you throw in the alternate close. *"Here or there?"*

Here are other examples

- *"Would you like the blue or the red?"*
- *"Would you like delivery this week or next"?*
- *"Will you pay on delivery, or shall we open a credit account?*

Questions can be tailor-made to suit your particular line of products, but remember that you must only use questions that the customer can reply to in a positive way.

You must learn to get your buyer in to the habit of saying *'Yes'*

In other words always give him the choice of two alternatives, both of which are equally advantageous to you. As soon as he says *'Yes'* he has bought. That's the alternate close.

The Problem Solved Close

This is always a good one to try. Use it when you are replying to a particular question about the product or your service. You answer with a close. It can be a bit cheeky, but said with right tone of voice and appropriate intonation, and in the right atmosphere, it can certainly work for you.

Your buyer asks you a question. "Can you deliver next week?"
You answer, "Do you want the order if we can?"

You might get another question something like "Do you do it in a larger size?" Your answer "Will you take it if we do?"

You get his approval and you write the order.

The "Throwing an Ace" Close

I will now give you some extra advice on closing. **Always keep at least one ace up your sleeve. Just in case you should ever need it.**

Just try leaving at least one of your product's important USP's for the final and concluding close. Then, if you get stuck you can always bring up this extra special benefit. Alternately you might leave a special concession or a special offer to get him to say "Yes" at the last minute.

The Bankrupt Close

I am mentioning the so-called 'bankrupt close' to get it out of the way. You should be aware of it, but I never want you to use it yourself. This close is only used by stupid or inept salesmen and that description does not apply to you.

This is what they do. They walk into a call looking down in the mouth. They will make their presentation, but will finish by saying. "Things are really bad for me right now. I have yet to book an order this week, and my Manager is on my back. I am hoping that you can come up with an order just to get me out of this jam."

A sad story isn't it? But make no mistake about it. It is a close and sometimes it will work. The problem is that it will only work once with any one customer. Try repeating this storyline and you will get booted out of the store. And you will deserve it. All God's children have problems, and that includes your buyer. He probably has enough problems for both of you, so never push your luck with this one. Never attempt to close this way. Ever.

My Favourite Close

I have left the best to last. This is the most positive and powerful close there is. It is the ASK FOR THE ORDER CLOSE. Even though many customers will not volunteer an order, no buyer has ever been offended by being asked to place an order, so you must never be afraid to pop the question. "If you don't ask, you won't get" is a good maxim, so there is never a reason to let a potential order go unasked for.

I have said it before, and I'll say it again. Your customer is in the business of buying. You are in the business of selling. You know it. He knows it. He will be expecting you to close so do not disappoint him. Be positive and just ASK FOR THE ORDER. If you don't, you will have no-one to blame but yourself.

POLISH THAT CLOSE

We have now discussed a few of the more common and basic closing techniques. There are many others, but with practice you should be able to tailor a close that suits you, your customer and the particular type of product that you are selling.

So we will now review some of those special skills that will enable you to give your chosen close a gleaming polish. That extra something special if you will, that will make you stand out as a positive and truly professional salesperson.

First of all I would advise you to really work hard on developing that all important sense of timing, and of knowing exactly when to ask for the order. Some salesmen instinctively know when to close; others will have to develop that perfect sense of timing and learn the hard way through trial and error.

And remember these important tips.

Never assume
I also want you to remember that as you work towards a sale you must always assume that your customer wants to buy. Become a Master of the Assumption. Be positive and *never* say anything that is likely to invite a negative response. Once you get him thinking in the negative you will find it extremely difficult to get him saying "Yes" again.

Don't ask him to buy
Try to avoid words like *purchase* or *buy*. These words only arouse thoughts of spending hard earned cash.

I also want to emphasis that you must keep putting positive questions to him. If you say something like "Shall I make this an urgent order?" you have avoided those dreaded words purchase and buy, but it means the same thing.

By the way, if you ask this question, and you get a positive reply – write the order – there and then.

Check your voice
Always check your speaking voice. Ask yourself – Is your story coming across in a clear, precise and believable manner? And another point, avoid at all costs, any temptation to gossip, **especially about your other customers, your competitors or their products.** If you do fall into this trap the buyer will be left to wonder what it is about him that you gossip to others about.

Avoid self-pity
Avoid, at all costs, any attempt at self-pity and always avoid inflicting your own depression or problems on to your customer. Just as you would have to do with a stage career you must learn to keep smiling through. The show must go on.

Never argue
Never be tempted to argue with a customer, even though you believe that he is wrong. You have heard the maxim *'The customer is King.'* It's true, so never argue with the buyer. If you do - you may well loose the order.   Not only that but you could permanently loose the customer as well. And you would deserve to. Therefore you will always be tactful and you will never tell him that he is wrong.

Instead, you will smile, you will be positive and you will say "Yes, others have thought that before until I was able to show them that…………………

Then you can go on to explain why things are different from the way that he sees them.

Never pre-judge
You will never pre-judge a customer or prospect. Even though it may take a great deal of time to really get to know the customer and his buying motives, you will never assume. Remember that even the smallest of shops may buy big. The best looking shops may be a credit risk. You can never be sure until you really know. Therefore you will treat every call and every buyer on its own merits and you will avoid projecting your own prejudices onto any business situation.

After closing
By the way, a very common but absolutely fatal mistake is to continue with your presentation *after* the customer has told you that he will buy. Should you miss that important 'buying signal' and carry on with your presentation, you could easily talk yourself out of the order. Don't develop a liking for the sound of your own voice. Once the customer has agreed to buy, you shut up – and let him do all the talking. Write the order.

Practice makes perfect
You have heard it said before, but there is no problem in repeating it here:-

Practice make perfect.

This is as true to selling as it is to anything else that is worth doing well.
The more you practice closing a sale, the greater will be your chances of success.

One final closing tip

I have one further tip that will help you to close in a more positive manner.
Maintaining the friendly relationship that you worked so hard to achieve is so important in closing. You could make the situation a whole lot easier if you post

him, about a week before your next scheduled call, some further product literature and a current price list. And don't forget to staple your business card to this information with a note to tell him when to expect you.

SUMMING UP
To sum up – *the only way you will ever get an order is to close the sale.*
You will close early and often. And you will use the close that is most appropriate to the situation.

You should be choosing between
- The Order Form Close
- The Puppy Dog Close
- The Balance Sheet, or Summary Close
- The Alternate Close
- The Problem Solved Close

Or, you will simply

ASK FOR THE ORDER.
And don't forget – make it easy for him to decide.

In the final analysis a salesman is employed to increase the turnover and profitability of his Company. This is true whether your objective is to obtain larger orders from existing customers or by obtaining new business.

Either way, when you really look at it, the Salesman's only job is to close the sale. Now you know how to do it. Just do it. Frequently.

CHAPTER 10

ANALYSE THAT PRESENTATION.

If you are determined to be a success you will have to learn to accept a degree of self-criticism and you must also be capable of analysing every single selling situation.

The best advice that I can give you is that, after ever sales call, you conduct a simple post-mortem examination as soon as practical. And that means even after a successful call, when you have come away with a decent order.

Sure it's absolutely vital to analyse that presentation after an abortive call, but even when you have managed to write an order, consider this. Did you get the order because you made a successful presentation or did you get the business **in spite of giving a poor presentation?**

Remember this. It's just as important to know why you have succeeded in getting the order as it is to know why you failed. Learn from every single sales presentation. Analyse and ask yourself "What went right?" "What went wrong?"

If you take the time and trouble to analyse your presentation in an honest and forthright way you will surely benefit in a big way.

So what I suggest is that as soon as practical after every call, you sit down with a pencil and paper. The best time is as soon as you get back to the car, and before you drive off to your next call.

Now take the time to ask yourself a number of searching questions.

Here is a check-list of the type of questions that you should be asking yourself.

Questions that need to be answered following a successful call

- *Did I get the best order that I could?*

- *Did I promote the right products?*

- *Did I promote the right products to the right buyer for the right season?*

- *Could I have achieved more?*

Questions that need to be answered following an unsuccessful call

- *Was he ever really a customer? Did the store actually stock my type of merchandise?*
- *Could he actually afford to buy?*

- Did I correctly assess the customer and his buying motives? Worse, did I sell on the wrong buying motives?
- What was wrong with the products that I mentioned?
- Did I see the real buyer?
- Did I adopt a good opening?
- Did I fail to answer any of his objections?
- What objections did I successfully overcome?
- Did I sell all the benefits?
- Did I forget to close?

Questions that need to be answered after every call

- Did I call at the right time? Did I choose the right day? Did I have an appointment?
- Was I fully prepared for the call?
- Did I have all the samples, literature, prices, delivery dates etc. to hand?
- Did I create the correct buying atmosphere?
- Was my general attitude and conduct correct at all times?
- Did I cover all the points that I wished to highlight?
- Did I ask questions?
- Did I make it easy for him to decide?
- Did I believe?
- What did I really achieve?
- How can I be more prepared for my next call?
- When is my next appointment?

All these questions will need an honest answer. Others may well spring to mind.

Do not waste any of your valuable time trying to lay the blame at someone else's feet. Especially after an abortive call when you might easily be tempted to blame external circumstances or even the customer for your lack of success.

Face up to the realities of selling. If you fail to get an order it's your fault. No one else is to blame. Accept the blame honestly and also accept the fact that if you wish to improve you skills it is absolutely vital that you analyse every call and question every sales presentation.

Every time.

Confucius said "A man who has made a mistake and doesn't correct it is committing another mistake".

Knowing what went right and what went wrong will dramatically help you to improve and develop your selling skills.

Learning from your mistakes and then putting what you have learnt into practice may be a very tough part of the learning process, but you will be better prepared for success next time you call.

And next time you will be ready for him – right?

CHAPTER 11

PROSPECTING

Any regular, meaningful, and profitable increase in the sales volume from your territory will depend on a continuous policy of opening and developing new accounts. There is no doubt about that.

However we must face some hard facts. However good your territory, nothing will be forever. Your area will always suffer from a natural wastage of existing accounts. You will continue to lose some business naturally and it could be from a whole variety of reasons.

- *A business could close down or go bankrupt.*
- *A business may become such a slow payer that your Company decides that credit facilitates will have to be withdrawn. In other words the account becomes a credit risk. You are subsequently instructed to close the account and future turnover from that business will be lost.*
- *The business owners may retire or sell up.*
- *The area/location is being re-developed.*
- *And, surprise, surprise, you may loose an account, or at least, some of this business, to your competition.*

On the other hand it will be expected that your sales area will show a healthy and steady, year on year, increase in turnover.

Consequently it is a fact that there is an ever changing scene in the market place, and you will constantly have to find a good percentage of new business every year just to maintain your current sales volume.

Some of this extra business must, of necessity, come from the development of sales from your existing customers, but it would not be realistic to rely on this. You will always be expected to grow your sales area and you will consequently have to devote an appropriate proportion of your time to finding new business from new customers.

And there are only three ways that you have of getting new customers

- *Cold calling*
- *Canvassing/Advertising*
- *Prospecting*

Call it what you like, it will have to be done.

However, once you have found a prospect, you should use your first call to learn as much about this potential customer and his store as is possible. In particular you will attempt to obtain some indication of the buyer's current attitude towards your company and its products. You should also ascertain what his buying habits and motives are. And what type of store it is, and how is the store laid out. All this is useful information that will help you towards building a more professional sales presentation that will suit his particular buying motives. And don't forget to use all your samples and Sales Aides.

The good news is that on your area there will always be a number of potential new outlets for you to get your teeth into. These outlets will include:-

1) Businesses that change hands

A business will change hands for a number of reasons. An owner may wish to retire or simply move to another area. Then again, he may be moving into a larger and better store. Whatever the reason, you could be in for more business if you keep on top of the situation and watch out for these changes.

2) Shops that change trade

What was once a café could now be a boutique? Keep an eye open. Nothing stays the same forever. And that is particularly true of the retail trade.

3) New Shopping Centres

The concept of the shopping mall, shopping centre or shopping precinct is 21st century retailing and is definitely here to stay. New shopping centres continue to be developed. The fact is that consumers like them, and the foot traffic they generate makes them an attractive proposition to progressive retailers. However the rent, rates and other overheads in shopping centres are comparatively high and these stores will always be looking for a range of high profit, high ticket items, as well as high turnover lines. Stay in touch with all new building developments and do not miss any opportunities of getting in on the ground floor. And you will find that in Shopping Centres stores change ownership quite quickly and often. Keep an eye open.

4) Shops being re-built

Check out all those new building projects both off and on the High Street.
Keep an eye open for all new shopping developments. Behind that building façade could well be an exciting potential new business opportunity for you.

5) Expansion

Watch out for any of your existing customers becoming highly successful, expanding and opening up further branches. If you and your products have been part of that success you have helped him to expand and in return any expansion of the business will help you to increase sales.

6) Competitive Accounts

A competitive account is a business that strongly features; supports, or stocks, perhaps even on an exclusive basis, the products or services of a major competitor. Never allow yourself to believe that a competitor's account cannot be opened by you. You might well think that your competitor is firmly entrenched, and is there in such strength that there is simply no business opportunity left for you. **Don't you believe it?**

Now if there is a Competitor's account on your territory, and you believe that it has the potential to generate good business for you, the answer is to call **and keep on calling**. Keep calling: even if you appear to be getting a frosty welcome: you will never know what the future has in store.

If you keep calling, are persistent, stay positive, and continue to work on building up a friendly atmosphere then one day his business will come your way.

Sooner or later one of three things could happen.

- *This prospect may find that his supplier has run into problems and cannot deliver.*
- *The Competitor, or his Salesperson, may have upset the customer for one reason or another.*
- *Better yet, consumer demand for your products reaches such a level that the prospect has already decided that he will need to stock your line of merchandise.*

So the moral is simple – keep calling.

However before you make a call on a competitor's customer; it is even more vital that you collect as much helpful information as you will need. Then just take a little extra time in the preparation of your sales presentation.

A few words of caution are in order here.

If there is a fairly large competitive account in the area, you would be well advised to weigh up the sales you could hopefully expect to achieve against any repercussions that the opening of such a large account would have on your present customers. If in doubt avoid upsetting your existing clients unless you are totally convinced that any fears on their part are groundless.

Also be very aware of any prospective customer that your competitor doesn't appear to want to service himself. This could well be the easiest new customer that you have ever poached from the competition, but just stop for a moment and think. How good is his credit rating? Is he buying from you simply because he finds it impossible to get merchandise or credit elsewhere?

You will have to be sure that you have the right reasons to start doing any business with this customer.

You owe it to yourself. You own it to your Company.

7) Old Customers

Yes, I am actually talking about ex-customers. Customers that you have stopped calling upon. Or customers that you thought were not really worth the time and effort.

But there could well be a golden opportunity here, and one that you could very easily forget or even overlook. I know that there are many salespeople who will tend to give a wide berth to ex-customers, usually through ignorance, often through embarrassment, or simply because they do not want to be reminded of a previous upset or mistake.

This is not the attitude of a professional salesperson. I agree that it may take a little more effort, diplomacy even, for you to get back into an ex-customer's good books, but such an effort can be most rewarding when it finally pays off, and he returns to the fold.

So, my advice is – just continue to call. However in your presentation be sure to highlight what is new, concentrate on the positive aspects of your Company and its products, and you can be sure that eventually something will genuinely interest him, and he will want to do business with you again.

Here is another thought. Who knows what you may find when you call on an ex-customer. You could well find that there is a new buyer in residence. The store's buying policy may have altered. The buyer may even be pleased to see you again.

You will never know – unless you call. You have nothing to lose, except perhaps a good order.

8) Non-stockists

Finally, and yet most importantly, there are the stores that are not currently stocking your type of merchandise. If you believe that your type of merchandise could well become a logical and profitable extension to the trade that is currently being carried in that store – then make a call.

TO SUM UP

With all these challenging opportunities you will see that you now have absolutely no excuse for not making sufficient time is planned for prospecting new business. And for obtaining that fresh lifeblood of extra turnover through the growth that every business needs for survival.

O.K. SO LET'S GO PROSPECTING

We will first re-cap on what we have already discussed. New business opportunities exist for you where:-

- *Shops change hands*
- *Shops change trade*
- *New branches open*
- *Shops are re-built*
- *New Shopping Centres are built*
- *There is a competitive account*
- *You can open an old or ex-account*
- *Stores that do not currently carry you type of merchandise.*

Quite simply you will have to be constantly on the look-out for every new business opportunity

It is all out there, you just have to keep looking and follow your leads.

As leads are going to be very important to you I would suggest that you devise a method of constantly keeping your fingers on the pulse of your territory.

You can start by building up a 'prospect file'. Somewhere to store all the information you gather and keep up to date. Then, as soon as time permits you will build every lead into your journey plan.

This is how you can increase your leads.

Vary your journey

The truth is that while you are developing a thorough knowledge of your territory you will find that you are gradually using the shortest and most practical routes between calls. This may be economic and efficient, but if sometimes you take an alternate route you may find some new opportunities. Varying the route you take between calls will not only relieve you of some of the boredom, but it will also add more interest to your regular journey.

You will certainly gain a more practical appreciation of the information than you have already obtained for your territory map.

Newspaper and Directory Leads

Studying all the local newspapers is another useful way of keeping up to date with likely prospects. Retailers opening new shops often like to do so with a splash. The chances are that they will advertise an opening in a local newspaper – and often such advertisements are supported by an editorial feature.

Remember that the local newspapers will give you a lot of information about local businesses. You will find many leads here.

Directories are yet another valuable source for leads that cannot be overlooked. Public Libraries will have a full range of trade directories that cover all the country's diverse trades and industries.

The classified telephone directories will also provide you with a list of leads. Take a tip from the Yellow Pages advertisement and let your fingers do the walking.

Of course all this information is now also available on the Internet. 192.com plus many other websites will provide you with a whole host of leads and opportunities.

Customer Leads

You will find that your existing customers could also be a great source of valuable leads. If you ask, you might find that they are prepared to supply you with some sales opportunities. These could be particularly valuable, as a third party recommendation will usually carry a lot more weight, especially when that recommendation has come from a respected friend or even a competitor who already carries your merchandise.

Other Sales people

And here is another interesting thought. Do you ever met up with the competitor's sales people, or even delivery drivers, while travelling your territory. Do you ever meet up with them socially? There's nothing wrong with engaging them in friendly conversation. They can tell you a lot, and some will. But make sure that it is *you* that lets *them* do all the talking. So, just listen and you will learn something. Whenever you are able to obtain an introduction from a third party that would be most helpful

One final thought on prospecting

You are already been cautioned about pre-judging a customer. This advice will obviously apply equally to a prospective customer.

Just remember, that however good a salesperson you think you are, do not expect to get an order on your very first call.

Don't be disheartened, stick with it and, provided you can establish that friendly atmosphere from the outset you will be able to return at a later date and progress the situation to a more positive conclusion.

You will also have to prove to this prospect that you are genuinely interested in his business, and that you will look after him and call on a regular basis.

By the way, a final thought on this subject. Even a prospect can sometimes come up with a third party lead.

Just ask him.

CHAPTER 12

OPENING A NEW ACCOUNT

As we discussed in the previous chapter, although the basic procedure is the same for all prospective customers, no two new accounts can be opened in exactly the same way. Therefore, you will have to acquire some basic information before you make any attempt to open up a new account.

You already know that you will greatly improve your chances if you make at least one exploratory visit before you actually attempt to sell him. The objective in making such an investigative call is to find something about the prospect that will help you in your subsequent sales presentation. Now before you make that very important first sales pitch you will be in a much stronger position to tailor make the presentation to the particular motives and desires of that individual buyer.

A useful exercise would be to ask yourself these two vital questions.

- *"Why would this person buy what I am selling"*
- *"Why would he buy it from me"*?

The way you answer this will give you some important indications as to the style of presentation that you should be planning for.

On your second and on each subsequent call you will be more adequately equipped to reach an agreement with the buyer on as many points as possible. While, all the time, continuing to work towards that final close and getting the order.

As you further develop your selling skills you will soon find that you have acquired sufficient ability to open a new prospect on your very first call. And then you will succeed in saving time as well.

But understand that we must always be realistic. Although you will, from time to time, open a new customer account on your very first call I do not want you to think that it will always be that easy. So do not be downhearted when an order fails to materialise as quickly as you would like. Just keep on calling.

Remember this – in the retail trade it will take a salesman an average of six prospect calls before a sale is finally made.

Keeping existing customers informed.

A very important ethical point to consider when opening any new account is to consider the ultimate effect that this action might have on your existing customers, especially those in the same locality.

My best advice is to adopt an 'honesty is best' policy and never shrink from telling your customers that a new account has been opened.

Explain to your customer that you would never have opened the account in the first place if you believed for one moment that this would have an adverse effect on his business.

Point out that greater distribution of the product will invariably bring major advantages to the consumer, and anything that is good for the consumer is likely to be good for his business too.

Bear in mind that if a customer hears the news from a third party it could well put you in a difficult position.

This could be particularly true if the informer is a competitor's salesperson. Your competitor might do his best to see that you and your company are seen in the worst possible light. And he might well take delight in doing so.

Therefore you will make sure that none of your actions ever gives your competitor that satisfaction.

There is another important point to consider.

If your company operates an exclusive distribution policy that restricts the number of outlets in a particular area, you should not be opening competitive accounts in the first place. So don't even consider it.

If, on the other hand, it is company policy never to offer exclusive sales rights, you would be wise to tackle this problem in a forthright and open way.

CHAPTER 13

OPENING AND CLOSING A CREDIT ACCOUNT

Opening a Credit Account

Every company should have its own policy as to how new credit accounts are opened. You will therefore have no choice but to follow those rules.

However, it is likely that, as the person on the spot, you will be the one to supply all the required information. At least you will probably be asked to obtain at least one Bank reference and perhaps two credit references, before you write that first order.

You will need complete details. Get the full name of the owner or owners of the business. Remember that the buyer may not be the owner. Then ask for all the Bank and trade references that your company requires.

If this situation is handled correctly, the customer will understand the reasons for good credit control, and will not object to your questions. You can say *"I'm sorry about all this red tape, but just for the record the folks at Head Office need this information."*

If you have the right attitude you will find that this exercise helps in gaining the buyer's confidence, especially if you need to mention that there is likely to be a longer than usual delay in processing the first order, as the references need to be checked and the credit account opened.

Finally, be sure to transfer all the information you have obtained onto the customer record card so that you are ready and prepared for your next call.

Is there a risk?

I believe that all professional salespeople have a firm duty to their employers to ensure that every prospective account customer is likely to be a good credit risk. Maybe you think that credit control is not your problem, but if you take a risk with your company's money, and bills are not paid, it might well be your problem.

If you ever have a doubt about someone's credit rating just ask yourself this simple obvious question. "Would I give this customer credit if it was my money"?

The clues are there. For example a well stocked store or warehouse that includes supplies from companies whose brands you are familiar with can indicate that the customer's credit is good.

On the other hand, if a potential customer appears to be carrying far too little stock for his needs, and you can see empty shelves, take care; this customer may be a poor credit risk.

One potential customer to always be on the guard against is the one that is trying to buy from you because your competitor has stopped supplying him.

Closing a Credit Account

If an account needs to be closed – close it. It's that simple. There is absolutely no point in shying away from taking these steps and there is never any reason for keeping a credit account open unless it can be totally justified.

Either the company or even the salesperson may decide to close an account for one or more of these reasons.

- The account has become a bad credit risk.
- The owners are generally considered to be poor business people.
- The account has become uneconomical to service because of the limited sales volume it can generate.
- The business is being run down.
- Your products are presented in a way that damages your company's reputation.
- The business has suffered a change of ownership that causes any of the points mentioned above.

If, for any reason, you have to close an account ensure that the trader fully understands the reasons behind that decision. If you just stop calling on him without telling him why, you may find that sometime in the future an unfortunate and embarrassing situation may develop.

CHAPTER 14

CREDIT CONTROL AND CASH COLLECTIONS

Every strong and progressive company will always have at its base a viable and sound credit control policy. Credit makes the retail world go round: and is essential to the successful operation of every business. Consequently anything that is so essential to good business practice has to be of vital concern to every single salesperson.

However, the policy of just how much involvement a salesperson should be expected to have in this aspect of the business will vary from company to company.

Many companies insist that credit control is the sole responsibility of the credit control department. That's fine. Their thinking is that credit control can get in the way of a salesperson's positive selling attitude. There is some merit in that policy, as a salesperson really does not need anything of a negative nature to get in the way of, or adversely effect, the overall sales situation.

On the other hand there are companies that take the view that the sales department has a duty and a right to get involved with obtaining all accounts that are overdue for payment.

I do not disagree this either of these policies. Companies must choose the policy that works best for them.

But, what I do believe is this. The whole of the credit control department, as well as all other company personnel that are in contact with customers, should be totally sales orientated. I'll go further. All company employees should be trained to be sales orientated. After all it is the profit from sales and only sales that actually pay the salaries of all the employees.

Any salesperson who writes an order should actually be demonstrating, by his very action, that he has confidence in the buyer from the point of view of his credit worthiness. Therefore whenever a salesperson accepts an order in good faith, and that customer subsequently becomes overdue with his account, the salesperson should not hesitate in bringing the problem out into open. There should never be any embarrassment in asking for an invoice to be paid on time.

By handling an overdue account in a diplomatic way, you will actually be doing your customer a big favour by helping him to keep his account open and his credit rating good. That's a fact.

CHAPTER 15

HANDLING COMPLAINTS

It is inevitable. No matter how hard you try, how hard you work, sooner or later, you will have to face, and then handle, a complaint or serious problem with one of your customers. Recognise this fact from the outset and be prepared to face up to the situation.

As you are a professional, the likelihood is that the problem will not be your fault, but if it does turn out that the error was yours, be totally honest about it and accept the blame. In full.

On the other hand, the problem could just as easily be caused by someone or something outside your control. A mistake may have been made by someone in invoicing or despatch. There are a myriad of ways that things could go wrong. The problem could also be simply a figment of the customer's imagination.

The real difficulty is that, although you may only be the salesperson, in the eyes of the customer, *you are the company*.

It is therefore your responsibility to sort out the problem, whether you like it or not, and you will have to resolve it out as quickly as possible, then re-establish that friendly atmosphere and, finally you will have to re-motivate your buyer into placing further orders with you.

Whenever you find yourself in this particular hot spot, you must go straight to the heart of the matter, and follow these basic principles.

- Be polite. Ask the customer to outline his problem and carefully listen (without interruption) to everything that he wants to tell you. I'll repeat that because it is so important. **Let him finish what he has to say, and resist any temptation to interrupt him.**

  Speak back to him, intervene or interrupt him while he is full flow, and you will find that every interruption you make will just add fuel to the fire. Every word that you utter will keep him going, reminding him of something else that has gone wrong. Argue with him, get into a row, and he will bring up other points that may have previously been long forgotten.

  Just let him go on, and on, and on. In spite of whatever he may have to say, even if you believe him to be totally wrong, resist any temptation to intervene. Stay silent, and you will be surprised to see how quickly he runs out of stream, especially if he is upset or angry. The quicker he gets everything out of his system the quicker he will calm down and be receptive to what he has to say. Remember the old adage,

  "A good listener is not only popular, but after a while he learns something."

You asked him to explain, so shut up and listen.

- Be sympathetic and, if you or your company are obviously at fault – apologise and admit the mistake. Honestly and sincerely.
- Check all the facts over with him, and, in his presence, write everything down, asking for any documentation or other evidence that may be available.
- Make a decision as to the action you are going to take. Tell your customer what you will be recommending your company should take, and what he should do.
- Take the action that you have recommended. Then follow it up.
- Go back to square one and take steps to regain the buyer's confidence.

There is one final and happy conclusion to this chapter. Recent studies have suggested that a very high proportion of people who complain are still content to stay with their supplier. Complaints are often made because the customer holds a high opinion of their supplier and he is usually quite anxious that genuine problems are properly aired and improvements subsequently made.

The only sure way to lose a customer that complains is to ignore him.

Therefore continue to look on the positive side and bear in mind that a well-settled complaint will invariably strengthen the bond between you and the customer.

Finally – remember that in reality the best way to deal with problems is to see that they never happen in the first place.

CHAPTER 16

THE WHOLESALER - RETAILER RELATIONSHIP

What's the Policy?
As a matter of policy some manufacturing companies and distributors will sell to the wholesale trade on a direct or an exclusive basis. Other companies will service the wholesaler as well as some or most of their retailer customers. Many distributors will directly supply both the wholesale and the retail chains of distribution.

Whatever the marketing policy of your company, you must be sure that you fully understand the rational behind that policy, and you must never allow your selling activities to prejudice that policy in any way.

Should it be your company's policy to supply product at both the retail and the wholesale level, it is also possible that you will have to operate a system whereby certain retail orders can be referred back, or 'turned over' to a local wholesaler. These orders are called 'Transfer Orders'.

Transfer Orders
Transfer orders are transferred over to a local wholesaler rather than being shipped directly from the manufacturer to the retailer. If you operate such a scheme you must never make the mistake of thinking that a small direct account is more valuable to your company than an order transferred to a wholesaler. If you take into account the costs of picking and packing, invoicing and delivery, etc. you should readily understand that small direct orders can actually be very unprofitable. The local wholesaler is usually better equipped to deal with these small, albeit regular, orders.

As soon as you first get a new, but comparatively small order you should ask the buyer if he already obtains some of his business from a local wholesaler and then ask exactly who that wholesaler is.

Should you discover that he does receive regular deliveries from a particular wholesaler then you should encourage him in continuing with that buying policy by taking a transfer order. This action will help you to gain the wholesaler's confidence and then he will be more likely to give you some extra support in return. Alternatively, by converting the retailer to a direct account you could just as easily make an enemy of the wholesaler. A major bugbear of every wholesaler is the supplier who expects him to carry a full range of products whilst, at the same time, continues to sell the retailer direct.

Buying Direct
If it is clear that your retail buyer has a genuine preference for buying direct

there is no reason why you should not discuss this openly with the wholesaler, and explain that you have taken an order and tell him why.

No wholesaler can honestly deny a retailer the right to buy directly from the manufacturer or main distributor, especially where the local wholesaler is not prepared to carry sufficient stock of your products to meet all the orders that are generated from the area.

It can be more profitable and economical for a company to supply wholesalers on an exclusive basis but this is only true when such a policy can give the product line the full sales penetration that is required. "Buying direct" only pays dividends if the local wholesaler is unable or unwilling to stock sufficient inventory to satisfy the demands that have been created by the supporting advertising and PR campaigns and by your own selling activities in the area. Consumer demand has to be satisfied one way or the other. And that is your ultimate responsibility.

What's best?

The primary objective is that consumer demand has to be satisfied. You must always bear in mind one further point whenever you are considering the economics of the wholesaler/retailer relationship.

And it is simply this. A wholesaler that orders for example, 100 units of stock is often giving you a better, and certainly a more profitable, deal than you would get from ten separate retailers each ordering 12 units direct.

The reason for this is that when a wholesaler's stock level starts to get low from let's say, 6 retailers ordering 12 units, the wholesaler may well order another 10 units to bring his stock levels back up to a healthy position.

The costs involved in providing extra discounts that the wholesaler will demand will always be more than paid for by the savings obtained in the cost of transporting orders directly to retailers.

A fine line has always to be trod when comparing the relationship between a manufacturer and his wholesale and retail customers.

Common sense as well as market forces will determine the ideal sales policy of each and every company.

CHAPTER 17

MERCHANDISING

Merchandising is no longer considered to be an auxiliary to selling. Today product placing and merchandising is a major factor in the ultimate success of every single consumer product sold in store.

Companies and individual salespeople now realise that it is simply not enough just to supply the goods they produce. The consumers have to be made aware of the product and a need or desire to own the item must be created.

National and local advertising plays its part, but every successful advertising campaign must be supported by positive, active and detailed sales promotion.

Both wholesalers and retailers need to be provided with this important back-up service, and merchandising is just one important method we have of helping to create a demand for a product and generate those vital extra sales.

Good merchandising needs special techniques, and nowadays many more people are currently employed to work in-store as full time merchandisers.

Whether or not your company employs such merchandise you will almost certainly need to gain some expertise in this field. Your sales may suffer if you don't.

Good merchandising includes helping and encouraging traders to join in national promotional activities. It also means better management of in-store space, and this is especially true where a supplier is trying to build himself a reputation for high quality products or services.

But merchandising really comes into its own when selling to the "Cash & Carry" outlet, and to the self-service retailer, and especially in those accounts that will allow you some ordering discretion.

Although your job is to sell, your sales targets will be more achievable if you can plan some form of merchandising at every one of your calls.

Remember – merchandising will help you to sell more.

Take every opportunity
Take every opportunity to merchandise your products in store. Bear in mind that your objective is to back up, or help develop, your company's advertising programme or, at least, its reputation for excellence. Indeed anything that you can do that will help the trader increase his turnover and profit margin will not only gain you the buyer's confidence but will also greatly increase your company's share of the market.

Create an impact
But, apart from increasing turnover, you must have one other firm objective in mind whenever you consider that a particular situation calls for some form of

merchandising.

Your objective? *To create an impact.* In other words to stop someone in their tracks and to direct their attention to your product, promotion or display.

Use the tools
There are many useful tools that can be used with effect to improve the profile of any product on display. These include:-
- *Racks.* One of the better merchandising concepts introduced in recent years is the custom-made product display or rack. These units have a wide range of advantages that bring benefits to you and to the customer in extra sales. Whenever products are displayed on these fittings, a good racking system will ensure that maximum turnover is generated. Imaginative displays will also create greater customer satisfaction, as the full range of products can be shown together. Whenever merchandise is laid out in this type of well organised and systematic style it makes for easier and faster buying.

  Display racks are best suited for a self-service or self – selection environment, where they can sustain and dramatically increase impulse buying.
- *Window Displays.* An attractive window display is yet another fine example of good merchandising. Once you have gained the buyer's confidence it is probable that he may allow you, for a limited or seasonal period, the use of his shop window for a special display of your products. He may be even keener if you offer to do the window display yourself and can demonstrate some expertise or knowledge on this subject. I am sure that there is no need for me to tell you just how effective this form of merchandising can be. Every window is a 24/7 salesperson that is working non-stop for you.

  Window displays are particularly well suited to seasonal promotions (Christmas, Spring, etc.) and also for new product introductions.
- *Shelf Talkers.* Shelf talkers are very effective in drawing the consumer's eye to a particular product or display. They are very simple, but they work, whether added to the shelf or the product itself. If your company produces them, use them.
- *Dump Bins.* Dump bins and random piles of merchandise dotted about the store are a great help in attracting a consumer's attention, and is a proven way of generating extra impulse sales. Random displays should also be used for highlighting new products and promotional offers.
- *Posters and Show cards.* If you are attempting to highlight special offers and promotions then these offers must be clearly seen. A showcard or poster could be the perfect answer. However the showcard must give the special price and at least one major feature of the product. Good examples are *new,*

improved, Introductory Price.

Keep it clean and tidy
Merchandising concepts can be as complicated as they come, or as simple as dusting. I say that because I would always recommend that you carry a dusting cloth in your briefcase. Then, should ever the chance present itself, you can take the small amount of time and trouble that is needed to dust, clean and rearrange your product display to make it even more effective. Always remember that nobody can be expected to be attracted to a dusty or dirty display, so do your own bit to keep all of your valuable merchandise clean and tidy. This too is all part of merchandising.

You should also remember that no matter how much consumer demand is created by your company's advertising programme, and by your own efforts within -store, in the final analysis, no-one is going to buy a dirty, damaged or unattractive looking package, or a product from a messy display. Do you agree?

What else?
You are a professional salesperson and therefore you will need to constantly strive to discover new and innovative ways of achieving maximum distribution for your product, and by securing and maintaining adequate shelf space within store or warehouse. Effective merchandising will also ensure that store personnel know how to handle displays and pricing that will show off your products to the greatest benefit. And this will also work to your advantage.

Therefore you must, at all times, watch out for opportunities and ways of obtaining more and even better shelf space within the outlet (or in a Cash & Carry warehouse).

You are proud of your products. Well, you must be, otherwise it would have been impossible for you to sell them with enthusiasm and determination. You should be just as proud to see them well displayed. If you have the correct attitude towards your products you will take every opportunity to improve, enhance and develop every in-store display. Even if that means simply keeping the shelves clean, tidy and well stocked.

- **And here is another useful tip. Experience shows that for maximum impact Thursday, Friday and the Weekend are the best days to launch a sales promotion campaign.**

Finally, don't forget to give seasonal lines that extra space during their own particular buying season.

Merchandising the Self-Service Outlet.
Whether you are dealing with an independent retail store, a wholesale

warehouse, or Cash & Carry, you must always aim at getting yourself involved in the way your products are actually merchandised or displayed within that outlet.   And, if that outlet is laid out on self-selection or self-service lines the same rules of merchandising will apply.

- *Check the foot-traffic*
  Check out the flow of the store's foot traffic, and see that, as the consumer progresses through the store, he reaches the more expensive products before he reaches those less expensive ones.

- *The best get the best*
  The first golden rule of "supermarket" type stores is that the best sellers belong in the best positions. Really fast moving lines are entitled to have the widest possible scope for promotion. It is absolutely fatal to try to promote a slow moving line at the expense of a flyer. It will not work, and could cost you dearly. Dearly, not only in terms of lost business, but also in terms of keeping the confidence of the buyer.

- *Positioning is vital*
  The correct positioning of each and every product is paramount. High-profit items should be displayed just about at eye-level. Research shows that as much as 80% of all products purchased are "reached for" whereas as little as 20% are asked for. Product displayed at eye-level will also sell more as customers are loathe to bend down, or go up on tip-toe unless they have no real alternative.

- *Display product*
  If shelf space is at a premium in the store, you could build blocks of products, with the smaller pack sizes put at the front of the larger sizes. If there is ample space, then aim at displaying as many facings of the product as possible and acceptable. A multi-facing display creates the maximum amount of consumer impact. If you are also able to alternate colours and sizes will be further helping to encourage consumer buying.

- *Impulse Lines*
  New, impulse lines should be grouped around regular impulse and every-day items, and in a place <u>following</u> their normal position.

- *Everyday lines*
  Every-day items, that is products bought out of need rather than impulse, should never be displayed in a prime or even an obvious

position. You should note how often, in a well-designed supermarket, how difficult it is to find such everyday products as sugar and flour. There is a very sound idea behind this thinking, and that is this. While a consumer is spending time looking for products that he actually needs, he should be constantly exposed to a wide range of products that he may buy on impulse.

Any amount of time spent on merchandising, whether it is from the simple action of dusting a pack, to the creation of a major in-store promotion, will be time well spent, and will ultimately pay handsome dividends.

I believe that every call is an opportunity for some merchandising. You will do yourself an injustice if you fail to spot those opportunities.

- *Fill the shelves*

  The next rule is to ensure that you completely fill the shelves with stock. However it is smart to allow just a few small gaps in the display to demonstrate to the consumer that there is some activity in the product's sales. Leaving occasional gaps in the display is also good psychology and sound merchandising. It leaves the consumer with the impression that other customers have already bought from that shelf, and often the consumer is likely to follow suit.

  Fully stocked shelves give an impression of freshness, whilst, on the other hand, an almost empty shelf conveys an impression that the best has already gone.

  I don't quite know why, but for some reason, nobody likes to pick up the last item from the shelf and, in fact, it is usually left where it is. Unwanted and unsold.

- *Rotate the stock*

  You must regularly check that store staff are correctly rotating your stock. You will also need to see that all recently delivered merchandised is placed behind, or under, older goods.

  Good stock rotation will also ensure that products never get stale, too badly battered, or simply past their "sell-by" dates.

  Never assume that your customer is properly rotating his stock. It will be in your own best interests to check it out for yourself.

Remember

You will not always get the chance to merchandise a store, but when you do get the opportunity, take it. Only you can develop a display that will

give your products maximum consumer impact. Many store assistants are far too busy taking care of the store to spare any time to keep your product line clean and tidy. On visiting a store, get dusting, display your products in an attractive and appealing way, replace any dirty or damaged products, and, if you can, gain extra facings.
A tidy, attractive display will always outsell a dirty, untidy display.
This is yet another way to gain some advantage over your competitors.

And that will help you sell more, as well as building a better relationship with your customer.

CHAPTER 18

AND FINALLY

Well that's it. This is the end of a very long, but I hope, enjoyable and educational journey through the world of selling. We have covered a great deal already, and you should have gleaned many ideas that will work for you to make you more competent, competitive and successful. The very fact that you have finished this course tells me that you are destined to become a top flight sales person.

But there is a lot more to becoming world-class in the field of selling.

Consequently I would still urge you to keep on learning, continue to develop those skills and remember that practice makes perfect.

But before I finally close, I will leave you with those all important sales persons rules of etiquette.

- FIRST IMPRESSIONS
  In dressing for the job be smart, never too casual. Men should ideally wear suits, not jackets and trousers. Dark grey, dark blue and pin-striped suits carry a strong message of success. Avoid brown – it alienates some people. Women should ideally wear a comfortable two or three piece suit and dress fashionably, yet conservatively. Power dress by all means, but try not to dress above or below the level of those you are meeting with.
- YOUR CAR
  Whether driving your own or a company car you will need to keep it clean and tidy. You never know if your buyer may need a lift. It is also your responsibility to have the tyres checked, car serviced and maintained according to the Car's handbook. Obey the rules of the road and keep to the speed limit. And remember this – if you lose your driving licence you may well lose your job. Be responsible.
- SMOKING.
  Simply don't. Smoking is now banned in most public spaces so restrict smoking to places where it is legal. You will never light up in the presence of a buyer, unless you are invited to do so as you will always assume that smoking is likely to cause offence.
- DRINKING.
  Another big no no. It's just not professional. Your customer may be teetotal or otherwise offended and you could lose the order. At best you are endangering your driving licence and your job. At worst you may slur your words. Drinking or any drugs for that matter, have no place in a selling environment.
- HAT OR CAP.
  If you wear something on your head, observe normal courtesies, and remove it as soon as you arrive on your customer's premises.

- *SWEARING.*
  Don't.
- *MEETING OTHER SALES PEOPLE.*
  Should you make a call and you find another salesperson already in the store, wait outside. It is
  unprofessional to hover in the background while another sales person is making a presentation.

I wish you every success in the future.

Prosper and enjoy every aspect of your career in sales.

www.ingramcontent.com/pod-product-compliance
Lightning Source LLC
Chambersburg PA
CBHW061514180526
45171CB00001B/175